Praise for *The Oth*

The non-judgmental way *The Other* ...ates, empowers, and informs parents about all aspects of infant care is remarkable. Most appealing is how the authors appreciate the diverse circumstances within which families live, and how decisions about how infants are to be raised such as where they can or should sleep...are decisions that belong only to parents and not to external medical or governmental authorities who don't know them, who dispense inaccurate generalizations, and who forget that the only power they have is what parents choose to give them. This book begins with who the human infant is and not with adult ideas about what society says they should be. The authors never forget that all families are different, so what is good or safe or appropriate for one family may not be for another. I am certain that many parents and babies will greatly benefit by the perspectives offered here.

> **~James J. McKenna, PhD, Director of Mother-Baby Behavioral Sleep Laboratory at University of Notre Dame, author of *Sleeping with Your Baby***

Megan and Miriam have created a hip, readable, accurate and supportive book about my favorite topics: moms and babies. This book is filled with common, practical, everyday wisdom that unfortunately has become almost obsolete in our medically dominated birthing and pediatrics models. It is a fantastic resource for the new mom who wants to do things a bit out of the box. Natural birthing support, breastfeeding how-to's, co-sleeping, natural diapering ---you'll find it all here! And it's just a little sassy, too, which makes it fun to read! Nicely, done, ladies!!!

> **~Aviva Romm, MD, CPM, herbalist, author of *The Natural Pregnancy Book*, *Naturally Healthy Babies and Children*, *Natural Health After Birth*, and *Vaccines***

The Other Baby Book is terrific! I wish that every mom, dad, grandparent, and community member would read it. It is friendly, uplifting, and easy to read. What an invaluable resource!

> **~Darcia Narvaez, Associate Professor of Psychology University of Notre Dame**

What a fabulous book! Megan and Miriam are like your super-savvy BFFs who have pounded the pavement gathering the latest research & practical guidelines, and written it up in a chatty, humorous yet authoritative format that will speak to NPR and TMZ fans alike. They artfully perform the deft maneuver of challenging the status quo…in a way that's engaging and empowering, rather than overwhelming. And sprinkled amidst this jaunty parade of exceptionally well-researched nuggets…is the lyricism of Megan's "A Novel Mama" interludes to whisper open the sweet soft spot of the heart.

~Marcy Axness, PhD, author of *Parenting for Peace*

The Other Baby Book brings utter relief, recognition and joy to mothering a baby. It is what every mother knows in her heart and doesn't dare to follow. Veteran mothers are likely to say, "Oh, how much I wish I knew this when my child was a baby." Reading it will leave a mother equipped with long forgotten and invaluable information, and empowered to be the mother she really wants to be.

**~Naomi Aldort, author of *Raising Our Children,
Raising Ourselves***

If you're searching for a parenting book that holds your hand and opens your eyes, this is it. Megan and Miriam have meticulously researched gentle, natural parenting practices, and the results are clear: the bond between baby and mother is of utmost importance. *The Other Baby Book* will help you push aside the cultural "shoulds" and practically embrace your mother's intuition.

~Linda Folden Palmer, author of *The Baby Bond*

Written with humor and wit, *The Other Baby Book* is truly a page turner. It gives new mothers the reaffirmation they need to trust their hearts—while grinning.

~Elizabeth Antunovic, Co-founder of Boba, Inc.

Kudos …for birthing an eminently readable, oh-so-practical, warm, nonjudgmental, well-researched book that I would like to see every prospective mother read before her baby arrives—and, more importantly, *every baby* would appreciate his mother reading!

~Nancy Wainer, CPM, author of *Silent Knife*

Being immersed in the baby planning/maternity concierge world I've read a plethora of baby books and *The Other Baby Book* is by far is the most refreshing, non-judgmental look at pregnancy and new motherhood.

~**Melissa Moog, Founder, Itsabelly Baby Planners,**
President, International Baby Planner Association;
author, *Itsabelly's Guide to Going Green with Baby*

A++! *The Other Baby Book* is a warm, practical and comprehensive guide for intuitively parenting your baby that enables you to tap into and celebrate your innate wisdom.

~**Laurie Boucke, author of** *Infant Potty Training*

The Other Baby Book would be a valuable and informative gift for grandparents, caregivers and friends who would benefit from learning more about natural parenting. Sharing this book is a perfect way to reassure, explain rationales for differences in parenting styles, and provides the opportunity for thoughtful and respectful conversations.

~**Nancy Holtzman, RN BSN IBCLC, VP at Isis Parenting**

…An energized book about pregnancy, giving birth and caring for your baby. It's a super read—light, informative and delightfully quirky.

~**Wintergreen, Director for Common Knowledge Trust,**
producer of Birthing Better with The Pink Kit Method®

The Other Baby Book is the perfect book for parents who don't follow "mainstream" parenting culture. Massaro and Katz tell it like it is, in a style that is enjoyable to read. This is definitely the kind of book I would share with my friends.

~**Susan Chanse, VP, Babywearing International**

The Other Baby Book…supports a strong attachment between mom and baby. If all babies were raised in this intuitive way, the positive effects on our entire society would be incredibly profound.

~**Julie Verfurth, ND and Owner of NaturoKits**

…A marvelous "back to basics" book.

~**Sharon Heller, PhD, author of** *The Vital Touch*

The Other Baby Book gently guides, candidly informs, and thoroughly inspires you to trust your instincts as you bond with your baby.
~Carista Luminare, PhD, author of *Parenting Begins Before Conception*

An easy and fun-to-read introduction to the most important topics in natural and intuitive parenting.
~Melinda Rothstein, Co-Founder and Executive Director of Diaper Free Baby

Unique, friendly and down to earth, this very fine parenting book will inform and inspire us all in parenting the next generation with love, connectedness, freedom and fun.
~Sarah Buckley MD, Author, of *Gentle Birth, Gentle Mothering*

Parenting can seem natural from a distance, but the truth is, parenting is *only* natural after you have prepared yourself along the way. I literally couldn't put the book down.
~Stephanie Neurohr, CEO, Writer and Producer, *Mother of 7*™ Motherhood DVDs

I'm a huge fan of mother-to-mother support, and that's what I like about *The Other Baby Book*. I'd love to see all first-time mothers exposed to natural parenting ideas in this friendly, mom-to-mom way.
~Jessica Kosa, PhD, IBCLC

Megan and Miriam have brought together a wealth of resources not found in regular baby books. This thought-provoking read is a catalyst for individual inspiration as mothers create a joyful and connected relationship with their babies. *The Other Baby Book* is a book I selfishly wish had been there for me. This book is truly a gift.
~Beth Bejnarowicz, IBCLC, PCD

Suppose everything you've been told about birth, feeding, diapering, and parenting was conventional, commercialized and just didn't feel quite right. *The Other Baby Book*...gives you the confidence to go with your gut, follow your instincts and bond with your baby.
~Lani Michelle, author of Boobie Time Blog

The *Other* Baby Book

A Natural Approach to Baby's First Year

Megan McGrory Massaro
Miriam J. Katz

Cover design by Sarah Georgakopoulos, 2012
Cover photo by Rebecca Smith, 2011
Authors photo by Misha Katz, 2012

This publication contains the opinions and ideas of its authors. It is intended to provide helpful and informative material. It is sold with the understanding that the author and publisher are not engaged in rendering medical, health, or any other kind of personal professional services in the book. The reader should consult his or her medical, health or other competent professional before adopting any of the suggestions in this book or drawing inferences from it.

The authors and publisher specifically disclaim all responsibility for any liability, loss, or risk, personal or otherwise, which is incurred as a consequence, directly or indirectly, of the use and application of any of the contents of this book.

Library of Congress Cataloging-in-Publication Data
The Other Baby Book : a natural approach to baby's first year / Miriam J. Katz and Megan McGrory Massaro ... [et al.]. — 1st ed.
Includes bibliographical references and index.
ISBN: 978-1475185423 (pbk.)
LCCN: 2011945032
1. (Parenting) 2. (Infants—Care and Hygiene)
Dewey decimal #2011945032
FIRST EDITION

The authors gratefully acknowledge permission from the following people and sources to reprint material in their control: Kelly Bonyata; T. Berry Brazelton; Katherine Dettwyler; Katrina Dyer; Three in a Bed © Deborah Jackson, courtesy of Bloomsbury Publishers Plc.; Jessica Kosa; Heather McCue; Copyright Permission from Sleeping With Your Baby: A Parent's Guide to Cosleeping by James J. McKenna, Ph.D., 2007, Platypus Media, ISBN: 1-930775-34-2. For more information, visit www.PlatypusMedia.com or call 1-877-PLATYPS (toll-free); John Seabrook; Copyright 1999. American Medical Association. All Rights Reserved.

To Mum, your extravagant love nourishes my soul.
To Dad, your unswerving confidence in me is my foundation.
~MMM

To Mom & Dad, all I am as a mother I owe to you.
~MJK

Contents

Foreword

Over thirty years ago, we were two young mothers who happened to sit next to each other at a La Leche League meeting. We were happily nursing our babies, blissfully unaware that this meeting would launch both of us on a path from which there was no turning back. Our lifelong journey is that of promoting a more conscious style of parenting. For us that means to be "awake:" mindful, cautious, respectful, and compassionate.

The school teachers in us liked to research, attend conferences, read voraciously, and share what we learned. Transferring that knowledge into the 'classroom' of the home was challenging, realizing that so many decisions we would make would have lifelong effects.

We wanted to answer this simple question: What parenting information was evidence-based, and what information was motivated by uninformed 'experts' who were making a fortune on promises of raising perfect kids?

The science in child development that has come out in the last fifteen years is conclusive and exciting. Parents who treat their babies and young children with loving, responsive care, who are empowered to follow their baby's cues and trust their instincts, are literally wiring their baby's brain for empathy, trust, cognition and the ability to self-regulate in stressful experiences. When we are encouraged to disconnect from another human being, most importantly a helpless, dependent infant, (i.e. "Don't pick up the baby because you'll spoil it"), we're on the slippery slope to creating lifelong insecure relationships that are at the root of many of our societal problems.

When we launched Attachment Parenting International (API) in 1994, we felt a compulsion to share with other parents the science that shows conclusively the critical importance of creating securely attached children. We knew that parent support groups were key to raising children in a culture that depends more and more on virtual information gathering.

Megan and Miriam are mothers who share our journey, finding each other through a support group, and strengthening each other through friendship and common goals. Like so many other parents, they've been transformed through their experiences and feel passionate about sharing their intentional style of parenting from an informed and genuinely sincere place. They have taken a very courageous leap to step outside the comfortable culture of never questioning authority, and invite us all to question everything! Whether you embrace all of their lifestyle choices or not, we can fully support and celebrate their commitment to make informed decisions through the lens of the attachment and their concern for the environment. Anyone who reads *The Other Baby Book* will be moved and educated by the well-written and well-researched information on these pages.

Dear Reader, we hope that you, too will "find your tribe" of like-minded friends, to empower and support each other in raising your precious children. Gandhi once wrote that to achieve real peace in the world we must allow children to "grow up in their natural innocence" surrounded by our love. At the same time we must teach ourselves and our children to protect our precious earth. We parents cannot do this alone, but through our combined strength, passion and our love for humanity we can and we *will* create positive change on this beautiful planet for future generations.

~ Barbara Nicholson and Lysa Parker
Cofounders, Attachment Parenting International
Coauthors, Attached at the Heart: Eight Proven
Parenting Principles for Raising Connected and
Compassionate Children

Introduction

Hey, Mama!

We're so glad you're here. Are you ready for an adventure? We've got drama and history, humor and how-tos, evidence and encouragement. This ain't your mama's baby book.

It's *The Other Baby Book*.

Our purpose in writing this new mama guide is to bring to life an often-forgotten truth: **a mother's instinct is the best resource she has to create a joyful and connected relationship with her baby**.

The estimated $100+ billion dollar global baby product industries would rather you buy into this prevalent myth: mothering is a burden to be relieved by modern technologies. Today's moms are pressured (know it or not) to believe that a crib, disposable diapers, formula and sleep-training books are baby essentials. But we'll give you the other side to the story, like any good friend would.

We've been overwhelmed by the volume and popularity of books that reinforce the status quo, touting baby-care practices that make mamas harden their hearts to their babies' needs in order to get the job done. We've compiled some *other* practices within these pages for you.

Picking up this book is a small act of rebellion against the mainstream, and it takes a measure of courage. Congratulations for considering the path less traveled (in modern Western societies, at least)! We assure you that each practice bears its own rewards through deepening and strengthening your connection with your baby.

At its core, *The Other Baby Book* is a journey back to basics, so you and your amazing baby can love that first year—together. We hope the following pages will be a catalyst for reflection and experimentation. Through eight chapters, written as if we were chatting it up at our local coffee shop, you'll find compelling research, time-honored traditions, accessible commentary and practical tips to empower your family.

The Gut Check: A Lost Art

Intuition is a fancy word for tuning in to your innate wisdom, your deepest sense of what's right for your baby. The intuitive powers of women, and especially mothers, are both awe inducing and incredibly helpful, though most of us underuse this power.

One of the easiest and most practical ways we access intuition as mothers is by doing the proverbial gut check—vetting ideas or information against the feeling in our bodies. As you explore which ideas to keep and which to cast aside, we encourage you to check in with your most valuable guide—your inner mama.

The Voices Behind the Pages

We're Megan and Miriam, friends and mothers to two beautiful little girls. We like to question the status quo. Some cultural "wisdom" didn't sit well with us, like leaving our newborns alone to ensure "independence" or feeding a quick bottle of formula to get the baby "used to it." So before our girls peeked their little heads into the world we took to the proverbial streets and researched our hearts out.

After our babies were born, we had even more questions. Thankfully, newborns are sleepy and like to nurse, so we had plenty of time to read and investigate. By the time our girls were six months old, we'd made some amazing discoveries and wanted to shout our findings from the rooftops: *moms need to be empowered!*

How did we manage to write a book, when most new moms struggle to wash their hair? We held "meetings" in a play hut at the playground while our girls chewed happily on dried fruit. Our office hours? Naptimes and bedtimes. Cell phones were indispensible for late night journal reading while our babies slept next to us in bed. Rugs weren't always vacuumed, and Megan gave up her cat because she kept forgetting to feed him. (True story.)

We were fortunate to have supportive families, and we refashioned our lives to make mothering our day jobs. But we know ours isn't the typical new mom experience. Since questioning the system isn't likely to show up on to-do lists that include nursing and brushing your teeth, we made it our mission to give others the opportunity to mother with babies as their top priority.

We're moms just like you. But we partnered with established experts—*Our Advisors*—for each chapter.

Our Advisors

How many lucky students get to work with their favorite teachers? Our work was informed by attuned parenting practitioners Naomi Aldort; Elizabeth Antunovic; Beth Bejnarowicz, IBCLC, CPD; Laurie Boucke; Lawrence Cohen, PhD; Mia Davis; Nancy Holtzman, RN, IBCLC; Jan Hunt, M.Sc.; Miriam Khalsa, CPM; Alfie Kohn; Jessica Kosa, PhD, IBCLC; Dr. James McKenna; Nancy Mohrbacher, IBCLC; Gill Rapley and Tracey Murkett; Melinda Rothstein; Nancy Wainer, CPM; and Dr. Janet Zand. They advised, critiqued and contributed to ensure that our work was current, accurate and worthy of publication. You'll find their names in the brilliant text boxes they've written. We're grateful to all those who helped bring this book to life.

Megan, A Novel Mama

There are ideals, and then there's reality. Living the life is often a very different story than dreaming the dream. In *Megan, A Novel Mama* I'll splash color on the pages between the studies and put flesh on the bones of theory.

Miriam's Coaching Corner

As a professional coach, I ask questions that help us understand why we do what we do. Meeting my baby enabled me to toss many old beliefs out the window—some instantly, some with a bit more resistance. In *Miriam's Coaching Corner*, I'll share tips to help you see past the beliefs we've inherited. This is your show, so you get to choose what to keep and what to toss.

Overheard...

One of our dreams for modern mothering is to restore the oral tradition of passing wisdom from mother to mother. So we short-circuited the system to enlist top experts: everyday moms. Hundreds of women from across the globe weighed in, and their compelling sound-bytes are featured in our *Overheard* sections. Our panel of mamas responded to our most pressing questions, some quite private in nature, but they bared it all to share their hard-earned wisdom.

He Said, She Said

For simplicity's sake, when you see "mother," read: primary caregiver—whoever that is in your household. Another technical note: all the baby pronouns are male. This is for clarity's sake, since mother is female.

A Note on Guilt

A discussion on parenting wouldn't be complete without some mention of guilt. We'll keep it simple: we trust you. We believe in the strength and intelligence of mothers, and we know that you want to do right by your baby and yourself. Every choice we make has pros and cons, and reflects our values. As women, we tend to feel guilt around decisions, regardless of what choice we make. So we ask you to read with an open mind, and to respect your inner voice.

The goal of our book is **not to have you adopt and master our every word.** If something doesn't resonate with you, no matter how many studies back it up, we encourage you to follow Emerson's lead: "Trust thyself—every heart vibrates to that iron string."

Beyond the Book

We could only pack so much of our research between these two covers. Good news: we've saved the rest for you, and it's live on our website! You'll find more articles, information, and a link to our virtual community! We'll see you at www.theotherbabybook.com.

Birth
bring forth new life

During pregnancy, we stand at the crossroads of the miraculous and the mundane. We honor the sacredness of incubating new life, while smiling at the absurdity of shoelaces, or shaving past our knees. As belly flutters morph into rib jabs seemingly overnight, we prepare ourselves for birth—an event that both terrifies and elates us, and summons every emotion in between. Yet birth is the most necessary and natural occurrence on our planet.

In our educrazy society, it's easy to believe that a stranger with a degree is your best authority during delivery. But long before diplomas, there were mothers, and there was birth. Journey with us as we honor the wisdom of our bodies: a mother's intuition that blossoms alongside our growing babies.

The best way to stay in touch with our innate power during birth is to know the lay of the land—who's running the show, what they believe about birth, and why they think the way they do. This insight can help you pick a partner who will support and respect your values from pregnancy onward. In the coming pages, you'll find a birthing prep-talk and food for thought about your baby's first hours. Then we'll tread where few birthing books dare—the changing world of sex after delivery.

Birth Day Prep Talk

Dust off your imagination for a moment. Humor us. Picture it: you've been given a one-way ticket to Uzbekistan, dated nine months in the future. There's no declining this offer, whether you've been longing to visit the land-locked Asian country, or can't even find it on a map. What will you do before you board that grueling flight? Stock up on peanut butter and jelly, since you can't find either "delicacy" abroad? Learn the language? (*What* is *the language?*) Secure friends to greet you when you land, or scout out a place to stay for those first few weeks in foreign territory? Chances are, you wouldn't just hop on the plane without at least a bit of preparation.

But first births often play out like an unprepared trip to an unfamiliar land. How much more relaxed might you be on your birth day if you spent some time prepping? Taking a holistic approach to birth preparation is like learning a few key phrases in Uzbeck before your big trip.

Priming to Push

There are entire volumes and classes dedicated to preparing your birthing body. Some practices are innocuous, some helpful, and some downright harmful. Many books are written by doctors who haven't actually had babies, and much of the advice you'll find is based on opinion, which in turn is based on cultural norms. We'll give you some ways to prep for the big day based on evidence, rather than current trends. Fashion is for handbags, not for something as sacred as birth.

Good grub. Your body is a temple. It thrives when nourished with the purest, healthiest ingredients. To stay in peak shape throughout pregnancy and into childbirth, it's ideal to consume a diet of whole, organic foods—fruits, veggies, legumes, whole grains, and natural sources of protein, including wild low-mercury fish and meat from humanely raised animals. Probiotics, mercury free Cod Liver Oil, and a hearty prenatal vitamin round out a powerful birthing diet. And don't forget your water!

Mind your posture. The way you carry yourself and sit can keep your baby aligned for an easy labor or send him running for the hills. Some tips to keep him in position: don't cross your legs, slouch, or recline with your legs up during pregnancy. Tough to do when you're carrying around extra weight, but the pay-off is worth it.

Core value. A strong core—including abs, back, pelvic, hip and gluteal muscles—is key to keeping your body in good working shape and preventing issues on the big day. If you're already active, chat with an instructor who specializes in pregnancy to discuss modifications. If nothing else, stretch the muscles of your hips, gluts, calves, and thighs until you can get down like our hunter-gatherer ancestors and squat.

Katy Bowman, a biomechanical scientist, says pelvic floor issues are usually caused by too much tension in the pelvic floor (due to a lack of bootie strength), not because you've shirked your kegel duties!

Another reason to get fit? Physically active mamas spend about half as much time pushing than less fit women.[1] We know—you're tired, you're nauseous, and you don't feel like it. But we can almost guarantee that you'll feel better after a walk than after watching another TV show.

Make like a fish. Did you know that swimming can line up your baby for the easiest possible exit?[2] The breaststroke and crawl open your pelvis, and the belly-down position encourages your own little swimmer to face the back of your pelvis rather than the front. The difference may look small on paper, but if the baby faces your front, you're looking at a longer, more painful labor.

Keep it together. You can stack the odds of not tearing in your favor if you forego being induced, and combine excellent nutrition, strong core muscles, and warm compresses during crowning. Push-friendly positions, like down on all fours or lying on your side, take pressure off the perineum during labor. Above all, deliver the baby's head in a slow, controlled manner. This requires an experienced birth provider who can help you through the process calmly, and apply counter-pressure while the baby's head emerges. The more gently he comes out, the less likely you'll tear.

Childbirth Education

The whole point of woman-centered birth is the knowledge that a woman is the birth power source. She may need and deserve help, but in essence, she always had, currently has, and will have the power.   *~Heather McCue*

When birthing wisdom was passed from mother to daughter, formal childbirth education was unnecessary. These days, mothers seek information and guidance everywhere—from the Internet, to the hospital, to fellow moms. Just over half of all first-timers choose to participate in some kind of formal childbirth education. If you enroll, it's important to know beforehand who's writing the curriculum, and what their goals are.

Many expecting moms take classes at their birthing facility. These courses may be the most economical on the market, but they often come with an agenda. Doctors and hospital personnel tend to teach you what they want you to know, and not stuff like how to prevent tearing or being induced. According to a national survey, almost 60% of women who took hospital-based courses reported to be less afraid of medical intervention.[2] That may sound like a good outcome, but perhaps a better outcome would be less fear of *childbirth.*

Needless medical interventions can be costly. And deadly. With about 1 in 3 U.S. moms receiving C-sections, the nation's maternal death rate ranks behind 40 other countries. Given the country's medical resources, that number's way too high. It's not a black and white issue though: underlying issues often cause fatal complications. A rising C-section rate, an early induction figure of around 40%,[3] and the medicalization of birth globally, play a significant role too. But information is power. Armed with the facts behind the myths, you'll be prepared to make the best possible decision for your family.

When to Get Started

Though many providers recommend starting childbirth classes at the beginning of your third trimester, if you can find a comprehensive course that looks at pregnancy holistically, it's best to begin early in your pregnancy so you don't miss out on valuable time when you could be practicing relaxation techniques and refining your pregnancy diet. (Sneak preview: lay off the Snickers.)

Course Catalog

Group courses that aim to arm birthing couples with techniques to work through labor without analgesia (mainly epidurals) include The Bradley Method of Husband Coached Childbirth and HypnoBirthing®. Each course has a unique focus, but all provide expectant moms with an overview of the birthing process and management techniques such as breathing and deep relaxation. Most courses use the same methods, packaged in different ways.

If you're looking for something a little different, check out Birthing Better with The Pink Kit Method. It's one of the more unique packages on the market. The Pink Kit is a skill-based curriculum, which means you internalize and practice skills, from opening your pelvis to prepare for delivery, to lessening pain through positions and touch. The kit offers a comprehensive education about your birthing body, so you know exactly what's happening on the big day.

Birthing Menu of Options

Home Sweet Home

Whether you own or rent, live in a bustling city, or dwell on a few acres of secluded land, let's romanticize about your pad. What do you appreciate most about the space? Some enjoy being surrounded by reflections of their preferences and values. Others cherish the company of loved ones. For a woman birthing at home, there's a heightened level of appreciation. During this stressful yet transformational time, she can choose who will support her in what ways, and how she prefers to labor.

But giving birth at home—without fancy medical equipment—is primitive, right? Actually, an overwhelming majority of the world gives birth at home, even in developed countries. Many Westerners are skeptical about the safety of birthing in their abode. Our fears don't pass the litmus test. A meta-analysis of low-risk pregnancy studies found homebirths to be statistically just as safe as comparable low risk hospital births, while using fewer interventions.[4]

Homebirth rates in Western nations like the U.S., Canada, UK, and Australia hover just below 1% of all births, with Denmark as a notable exception: 34% of Danish moms birth at home. The tide is turning, though. From 2004–2009, Australian homebirths were up 33% and American homebirths were up 29%. [5] Modern moms are increasingly reclaiming the right to birth locally and naturally.

Overheard...

I wanted a supportive provider and a comfortable environment. So I chose to have my first baby at home with an incredibly skilled and patient midwife. It was the most peaceful, glorious, intense experience.

~Brianna, mom to Siley, Elise, and Kiera

Midwifery at Home. Midwifery views birth as a natural event and considers the entire cycle—conception through delivery—a normal part of life. It treats moms holistically. Practically speaking, midwives counsel pregnant moms on nutrition, emotional health and exercise.

Midwifery encourages moms to be active participants in labor and delivery, and most midwives shy away from getting credit for "delivering" babies. Instead, they recognize that mama is the one bringing her baby into the world and that midwives are simply "attending" births, and "catching" babies.[6] When asked how many babies she's delivered, Miriam Khalsa, CPM says, "Two, but I've caught hundreds!"

Midwives are trained to offer extensive preventative care to prepare mom for her best birth. While there can always be surprises during labor and delivery, births attended by midwives result in fewer C-sections than births attended by OBs.[7, 8]

When shopping around, you'll find there are different types of midwives, and the differences boil down to their training and scope of practice. Some midwives are unlicensed, but many have had formal, accredited training. In the U.S., Certified Nurse Midwives (CNMs) usually work in hospitals or birth centers, and have Master's Degrees in nursing and midwifery. Certified Professional Midwives (CPMs) go through extensive training and internship programs and are well prepped for homebirths.

Despite the rumors, it's not illegal for a woman in the U.S. to give birth at home. But some states have made it illegal for certified midwives to attend homebirths, leaving no legal protection for Certified Nurse Midwives who attend births in private homes. American mamas can check out the Midwife Alliance of North America's database of laws to see where their state falls on the issue.[9]

The Birthing Center

Birthing Centers can be found around the world, and are regaining popularity among moms in developed countries because of their home-like environment, often coupled with access to medical facilities. Most of these delivery spots are affiliated with hospitals. In the U.S., these partnerships generally mean health insurance will cover your birth. It also means more control is in the hands of the hospitals, so you're likely to be transferred if any perceived issues arise.

Overheard...

I birthed three babies at a birthing center, an old house. During my third labor, I wasn't progressing, so I went to the kitchen to make a snack while my husband napped. My midwife made me a bagel and sat down to chat about my plans for the weekend.

There were no flashing lights, beeping machines or nurses rushing in and out of my room. Just two "friends" chatting cosily...waiting for a miracle to come into the world.

After our baby boy arrived, the joy of delivering at the center continued. My husband was encouraged to snuggle in bed with me and our baby, as the baby learned to nurse for the first time. Five hours after birth, my older boys came to visit. All of us fit on the bed, and our family was complete.

~Kasha, mom to Brayden, Luke, and Adam

You won't find pain meds or surgery tables at a Birthing Center, which is why many moms opt in. The space is usually warm, inviting, and homey, and often the staff gets to know you and your partner before the birth day. Families are welcome to participate in the experience, and few restrictions are placed on laboring moms.

The Hospital

Hospital birth is the default option for the vast majority of Western mamas. We admit—it's pretty easy to sign up and call it a day. There are benefits aside from convenience and preventing your parents from freaking out, especially for women with health issues that may complicate birth. The top reason most moms cite for having a hospital birth is immediate access to emergency care, if needed. Also, pain meds are easily available for those who want them. But the other side to the story, the one Somewhere City Hospital doesn't advertise, is that increased odds of unnecessary interventions is a key contributor to a traumatic birth.[10]

You wouldn't wear a wool sweater to the beach in July, "just in case," would you? The average U.S. birth is no exception. Speeding up delivery with drugs, widening the exit, and C-section surgeries are on the rise and are performed on millions of moms every year,[11] when a simple dose of patience could do the trick.

But with limited beds and staff, hospitals gotta keep it movin'. Though there are exceptions—and we encourage you to seek them out if you want a hospital birth—birth is a business, and the more customers hospitals serve, the bigger the earnings.[12] Because there are only so many beds, some laboring moms are told to go home if they're not far enough along, which may actually work in mamas' favor. The anxiety caused by being in hospital can inhibit the production of hormones and slow labor even more!

By nature, hospitals are places where most patients are sick, so infections or complications can arise. And if you're modest—forget it. In bustling hospitals, there is very little privacy, with folks like doctors, lunch deliverers and photographers knocking on your door at all hours. Most tiring, however, is that moms often have to assert their wishes to keep their newborns close.

There are bright spots, though. Some hospitals, especially smaller ones, are more personal, baby-friendly, and mother-respecting. A good hospital is worth the work to find. Check out stats like C-section rates, attentive midwives, and glowing recommendations from moms who share your birthing values.

Birth Days: The Waiting Game

Many moms are induced if they've gone too far past their estimated due date (EDD), as if it were an expiration date. But for first time moms especially, this date is not written in stone. Healthy babies can arrive anywhere from 37-42 weeks! When we trust that babies know how long they need to bake, we can follow their lead on the exit plan. We've been coming out on our own since the dawn of humanity.

Obstetrics. The field of obstetrics developed from within a medical model, and specializes in caring for pregnant women with diseases or complications. While in the field's early days obstetricians (OB) managed "high-risk" mamas, present day docs attend 90% of all births—most of which are healthy, normal pregnancies.

Prenatal care with OBs seems to vary widely. Some adopt a more holistic approach, and others leave the vitals checking for nurse practitioners and make a cameo for the ultrasound. One study found the average OB prenatal appointment to be 5-7 minutes long.[13]

These doctors come with all the benefits of their rigorous education...and all of the drawbacks as well. As far as the actual birth day, OBs view labor with a cautious eye, and prepare for the worst—which usually doesn't happen. Moms are often monitored closely, and irregularities are addressed immediately. For some mamas, the careful obstetrician approach is a lifesaver, and they couldn't be more grateful.

The bottom line: we're not encouraging you to ignore your doctor's recommendations, but we are suggesting you vet your doctor's approach carefully before making a choice. When you're in sync and of like mind with your caregiver, birth can be an empowering and beautiful experience for mom and baby.

Overheard...

I developed HELLP syndrome in labor, a rare variant of pre-eclampsia. I asked if it would be safest to do a C-section, though I wanted to avoid one at all costs. My OB said no, my body was doing exactly what it needed to do; there was no reason I couldn't proceed with the birth I wanted. She said, "In your Hypnobirthing materials it says, 'I am prepared to calmly face whatever direction my birthing may take.' That's what you need to do now." I still tear up thinking about it—how incredible to have an OB convinced of women's natural ability to give birth.

I was restricted to lying on my back with an IV, but even so I had a wonderful, drug-free birth. I'm so grateful that I chose an OB known to support natural births.

~Heidi, mom to Sam

Midwifery in the Hospital. If a hospital birth seems like the best fit for your family, we get that. We both had our first births in hospitals: one with a midwife and one with an OB.

Overheard...

In my hospital room my nurse dimmed the lights, set up faux candles and put warm washcloths on my forehead. I hadn't requested these, but they really helped me relax!

~Tricia, mom to Kylie and Mason

If you chose a midwife for your hospital birth, you'll likely see a Certified Nurse Midwife (CNM). While quality of care ranges, midwives tend to spend more time listening to expecting moms, discussing concerns, and coaching nutrition, exercise, and other health issues. This hands-on care isn't just warm and fuzzy; it's preventative. Low birth weight is significantly reduced by this comprehensive model of care.[14]

Birth Doula. Thinking you'll need some girlfriend support on the big day, but don't want to wig out your BFF? Enter the birth doula. Doulas are professional labor coaches who are trained to understand the physiology of pregnancy and birthing. Perhaps unlike your gal pal, they get that you'll probably poop during labor. And they'll take it in stride. Doulas aren't going to look at you with wide eyes if you scream or swear, or yell at your husband for getting you into this mess. They're sympathetic to the emotional roller coaster thing. In fact, doulas are trained to help you better communicate with your partner, who they support, as well.

If you're interested in finding one of these godsends, ask around for recommendations early on in pregnancy. Typically doulas are hired by birthing families in the first or second trimester so that everyone can get to know each other before the big day. Another perk of hiring a doula is that she never goes off-shift. Unlike your favorite nurse who may go home right as you hit transition, your doula is in it to the finish, translating your grunts and telling that annoying nurse to stop snapping her gum.

While doulas can support moms in any birthing environment, they're especially helpful at hospital births when moms want to avoid unnecessary procedures. They'll interpret medical jargon, and guide you through the pros and cons of every stage. While many think doulas are only for natural births, they can improve experiences of moms who opt for meds or intervention too.

Overheard...

Our doula was a tremendous support to both me and my husband during the final stages of labor. We especially appreciated her help with immediate skin to skin and nursing during that first hour. Our baby's blood sugar was low after birth and had our doula not helped us nurse right away, my girl would have been sent to the NICU for formula per hospital protocol. We were so thankful that didn't have to happen! We're definitely using a doula next time around.

~Katie, mom to Annie

Postpartum Doula.   If you don't live with your parents—and most of us don't—there are other ways to ease the transition from one and a bump to full-time mama mode. Postpartum doulas schedule in-home visits with moms for days, weeks, or even months after the birth of the baby. Their schedules are usually flexible, and they support postpartum adjustment, parent-infant bonding, newborn care, feeding and development. Doulas can also help with meals and light housework, including that endless pile of newborn laundry.

A postpartum doula isn't just a glorified housekeeper or nanny, though. She's skilled in "mothering the mother." Sometimes we need to vent, shower, or figure out how to latch a sleepy baby. A skilled postpartum doula can support you through all of it.

If you don't have built-in support after the birth of your baby, you may want to hire a postpartum doula. Some governments or insurance companies pay; some moms shell out the cash, others ask family and

The Value of Postpartum Support

By Beth Bejnarowicz, Postpartum Doula, IBCLC

The saying goes, "It takes a village to raise a child." Instead, it's more helpful if the village takes care of mom and family, so the parents can raise their own child.

Sometimes we don't live in a "village" though, and other help is necessary. By gently encouraging new parents and protecting the sacred family circle, doulas meet parents where they are in their journeys. Many studies confirm the value of postpartum support.

Having a doula…
- Reduces postpartum mood disorders up to 50%[15]
- Increases breastfeeding rates[16]
- Empowers mom to gain confidence and self-esteem[17]
- Gives non-judgmental support and companionship
- Helps the parents achieve their parenting goals
- Enhances mothers' ability to nurture their family[18]
- Gives mom more time to bond with her newborn
- Frees up mom to enjoy her other children

friends to give money toward a few weeks with a doula in lieu of shower gifts. Additionally, you may be able to find a doula-in-training to work for free.

Pain Management: Back to Basics

We all know that epidurals can help us manage pain during the birthing process. Birthing classes aside, some of the simplest and safest options get the least stage time. We'll highlight our top picks.

Belly Breaths

If newborns could speak, they might offer you an important tip for labor: breathe into your belly! We all begin life taking deep abdominal breaths, and gradually become chest breathers as we grow. By the time

---

ABDOMINAL BREATHING EXERCISE

Put one hand on your belly and one on your chest. Breathe in through your nose, allowing your breath to expand your belly with air. Exhale through your mouth, pushing out as much air as you can. Deep abdominal breathing can help keep laboring moms relaxed and focused as they move through labor, contractions and delivery.

---

we're adults, belly breathing usually needs to be re-learned. It's a simple but powerful technique that can infuse us with a sense of calm.

Did you know that shallow breathing creates anxiety?[19] It's no wonder then, in a country where anxiety is a growing epidemic, that most Americans are chest breathers. We take quick, shallow breaths, barely filling our lungs. While it may look like we're taking a full breath when our chests puff out, deep abdominal breathing actually opens the lower part of the lungs where the most oxygen can be exchanged. When you breathe deeply, your muscles relax, your circulation improves, and oxygen moves more easily throughout your whole body.

Overheard...

It helped me to breath deeply while picturing the pain with a purpose. Each contraction allowed my body to open further in order to welcome the newest member of our family. By the third time around, I was able to embrace each contraction and tried to "enjoy" it knowing it would be my last birth.

~*Kasha, mom to Brayden, Luke, and Adam*

Picture This

Hypnosis is becoming a popular form of natural pain control for labor. The technique involves focusing on breath and creating a soothing mental image. Since pain is experienced in your brain, focusing your mind on a relaxing image during labor can bring pleasure...or at least a reduction in pain.

Like other pain mediation techniques, practice increases the effectiveness of self-hypnosis, namely the ability to clearly conjure and maintain focus on a mental image. Some laboring moms bring recordings of relaxation and self-hypnosis techniques, which can help them stay focused during the physical and emotional stress of labor.

Pressure Perfect

Massage has tremendous benefits during labor, but it tends to get little stage time in childbirth classes. The right touch can ease the stress of labor, stimulate contractions, and promote general relaxation and release of endorphins. As an added bonus, massage often eases pain, muscle tension, and fatigue.

Some women prefer to be left alone entirely once contractions have begun (as in, *stop talking, turn off the lights, don't breathe, and definitely don't touch me or I'll kill you*), and others appreciate massage or loving touch between their contractions.

A laboring woman's partner is advised to ask where she'd like to be massaged, and to meet her needs, including the need for space! Popular spots for birthing massage include the back, thighs, stomach, and hands. Again, practice makes perfect, and what expecting mama doesn't want to be pampered during pregnancy? So tell your partner to put down the remote and start rubbing!

When You're Wading Around

Water has become a hot birthing topic in recent years. Gisele Bundchen, supermodel and wife to NFL quarterback Tom Brady, birthed her son in her bathtub at home. Many mothers report that laboring in the water provides relief from contractions and aids in relaxation. Just 20 years ago, water labor wasn't an option at birth centers or hospitals, but today more than 70% of birth centers and about 50% of hospitals have labor tubs, and some even have birthing pools for a water delivery. It helps to consider how you might want to use water during your birthing experience, and then find out what options are available.

Labor tubs are simply that—tubs women can labor in. They are typically smaller than birthing pools, and are not intended for the actual delivery of the baby.

WHAT'S SO WONDERFUL ABOUT WATER BIRTHS?

- Emerging into water offers babies a peaceful transition from womb to world
- Hydrotherapy reduces pain during labor, especially in the lower back
- Moisture makes breathing easier, and can lower your heart rate if you're anxious
- Warm water softens the vagina and perineum, resulting in fewer tears
- Water reduces gravity, making laboring moms feel lighter and conserving energy

---

Birthing pools are deeper and larger than labor tubs, and take more time to fill and monitor the temperature. Pools are usually more comfortable, and large enough to fit more than one person, so they're ideal for labor and birth. Many home-birthing mamas rent birthing pools for their delivery.

Interventions and Intercessions

These words may look similar at first glance, but their practice and implications are worlds apart. The vast majority of mothers need support during birth. The degree of assistance can range from continual hands-on help, to occasional cheerleading. On one end of the spectrum is intervention. Think: a helicopter parent hovering over the laboring mother worrying and undermining by *doing to*. On the other end of the spectrum is intercession: a quiet, gentle parent, observing and empowering by *doing with*.

We recommend you choose a birth provider who is patient enough to allow you to listen to your body, and skilled enough to know how to work with the situation at hand. While issues that crop up during labor can have the same root whether you're in a hospital or at home, the way they're addressed can mean the difference between a traumatic or an ecstatic birth.

Get Your Motor Running

Sometimes caregivers in a hospital decide you're moving along too slowly. Many docs intervene if your bundle hasn't arrived by the EDD;

others may worry about mother or baby's health issues. We'll discuss some common medical interventions in the upcoming pages.

The Pits

Pitocin. It's known as "the pit." And moms who've been there say it's appropriately named. Scientists developed this synthetic form of oxytocin to jumpstart or "augment" labor. Pitocin is clearly overprescribed—some sources claim as many as 80% of women are given this potent drug at some point during their labor. But if your cervix isn't sufficiently ripened, the pit is far less likely to work.[20] Instead, you may just feel intense pain and longer contractions, which leads to an epidural…and also causes fatigue, which can result in mom being unable to sustain labor, ending in a C-section.[21, 22] Talk about a downward spiral! It's important to understand where your body is in the birthing process in order to avoid unnecessary interventions.

Pitocin is not without side effects to mothers. The manufacturer of Pitocin lists blood clots, brain hemorrhage and uterine rupture among the scarier adverse reactions.[23] The major risk of this potent drug, however, is to your baby. It's notorious for making contractions come hard and fast. And babies are often unprepared. Increased pressure during contractions can compress your baby's umbilical cord, which results in a decrease in oxygen supply. The FDA insert on the drug warns: effects are not limited to the birth day. Pitocin can create changes in babies' central nervous systems that show up as they grow.

Mamas on Pitocin can't rest on a birthing ball or relax in the tub. For your safety, care providers will keep you under close wraps with an IV, and your uterus will be monitored to make sure the contractions aren't so strong that your uterus ruptures. Baby's safety is crucial. His heart rate will be monitored either abdominally or with an electrode that penetrates his scalp skin. (Some babies end up with small scars on their head from the procedure.) If this doesn't sound like an empowering birth experience, we encourage you to discuss this intervention before the big day, in order to understand your practitioner's take on when (and *if*) it's appropriate.

But what about when Pitocin *is* necessary? Though most midwives would say the circumstances are few and far between, they do exist.

Babies who are awkwardly positioned and not responding to more gentle measures, and moms with health issues, may merit Pitocin.

Speedy Lube

Prostaglandins are like the key in the ignition of your car—they get things moving. More technically, they're a group of substances that control hormone regulation. And if you know anything about pregnancy, you're privy to the enormous role of hormones in the process. (Your partner really didn't mean for you to cry when he suggested the lasagna was a smidge on the cold side…)

Providers who want babies to come sooner rather than later may suggest prostaglandin gel to speed up the process. It will invade your privacy a bit though, so be aware. The gel is put into your vagina to help soften the cervix. Remember, semen does the same thing. The jury's out on whether the prostaglandin concentration is high enough,[24] but many moms stand by a little pre-baby intimacy to jump-start their labor. The difference, however, besides latex gloves and awkwardly avoiding eye contact with a stranger, is that prostaglandin gel has side effects. Diarrhea, fever, and fetal distress due to uterine hyper-stimulation (meaning contractions can last as long as ten minutes!) top the list.[25] Hmmm…even if you don't orgasm, sex is bound to be better than that!

Naturally Speaking

Babies have been born since the dawn of humankind, and left alone, the vast majority will continue to do so without any "help." If you sense your caretaker is trying to hurry a labor that just doesn't need to be hurried, before spouting a heated "Step off!" or wearily succumbing, you might consider some of these natural ways to get things going.

Alternative therapies. Acupuncture, herbs, massage, and homeopathy work best if you start weeks or even months before your due date. Make sure you're seeing a licensed practitioner!

Sex. Orgasms release your oxytocin, which starts contractions, and semen contains prostaglandins, which soften the cervix. Nipple stimulation also gets oxytocin flowing.

Movement. Walking or even changing positions can stimulate your baby to get moving.

Castor oil. It may or may not work, but beware: taking this old-school oral laxative often leads to vomiting, diarrhea and major cramping.

A Cut Below the Rest

Snip, snip to your lady parts. Shuddering yet? An episiotomy is a painful surgical cut along the perineum and rear wall of the vagina. If an obstetrician doesn't think the baby can make headway during the second phase of labor, they'll perform this "minor" procedure. Thankfully, due to research showing little to no benefit, the practice has slowed significantly in recent years. In 1979, 61% of all moms who delivered vaginally could expect to have an episiotomy, but as of 2008, the rate dropped to 12%.[26] Our vagina is incredibly adept at healing, and even a bad tear is preferable to cutting through muscle. Episiotomies can be done if the baby needs to be born ASAP to prevent injury or death.[27]

The Price of Pain-Free

Most women have one major fear in childbirth: pain. Other more dangerous, life-threatening complications seldom enter the picture. In our eagerness to block unpleasant experiences, epidurals have become the most popular form of childbirth pain management. In 2008, about 61% of U.S. mamas who delivered vaginally used an epidural.[28] If all goes well, you can remain fully conscious, and pain is limited or absent. For women with particularly long or exhausting labors, the epidural may give them the chance to sleep between contractions.
According to the World Health Organization (WHO), a normal labor that has been treated with an epidural can no longer be considered "normal." What some women find out—often when it's too late—is that epidurals require continuous monitoring, and you're usually stuck

Miriam's Coaching Corner

Ever wonder why horror movies are so popular? Or turn on the evening news and ask if the world is really as crime-ridden as it seems? The truth is, American culture consumes negativity like greasy potato chips—once you get hooked, it's hard to put the bag down.

Stories help us learn how to live. Oral tradition from the beginning of time has been used to pass on both wisdom and warnings. Birthing, especially in recent generations, is no exception. Pain and distress are tightly woven into our cultural narrative of birth. So is it any wonder that many of us are terrified to give birth? It's easy to hand over the reins to fear.

Fear-based decisions don't usually bring satisfying results. Control is an illusion, and when we make choices out of fear, we usually end up in a stuck place. Epidurals are a common tool we use to control birth, yet they control us entirely—pinning us to our beds as if we were ill. You'd never know we were about to perform one of the most powerful and miraculous acts of our lives.

When we set a specific intention for what we want to achieve, it's easier to overcome the fear. For example, you might say: When my baby enters the world, he will be embraced instantly with love. So, to realize your intention, where and how would you choose to give birth? What types of interventions would you use or avoid? While you outline your plan, make note of what fears arise, so you can address them, one at a time.

So how do you face down your fears? As you consider each fear, keep asking "and then what?" until you uncover the very worst of what's at stake. In the end, you may find yourself saying "so what?" But you won't know until you dig deeper.

in bed. But freedom of movement isn't just helpful for a trip to the vending machine (which, by the way you can forget—once the needle's in, no food for you!). Movement actually helps labor progress, and gives your baby a boost on his way down the birth canal.

Epidurals make pushing comical. You can't feel the baby coming out, which was your goal of course, but that also means…you can't feel your vagina. When the nurse says, "Keep doing that!" you may have no idea what "that" is.

Conversely, if you need to push in a different way, you'll often have little control over your muscles. Other fun side effects include the slowing of labor, which might not be bad if you're trying to get in a full 24 hours of *Lost*. But slowed labor means your likelihood of forceps or vacuum, or a C-section, increases. Postpartum headaches or backaches are not uncommon either. Think the epidural only affects you? Not quite. Epidural babies are often drowsy and may have trouble latching and sipping colostrum, those first drops of super rich immune-enhancing milk.

Under the Knife

While the traditional method of delivering a baby is a vaginal delivery, Cesarean sections, or C-sections, have been performed for hundreds of years. A C-section is a surgical procedure that cuts into the abdomen to remove the baby from the womb. Docs and mamas were glad when the technique was perfected. It was a lifesaver—literally: C-sections were first performed to save babies in mothers who died during childbirth. But as hospital births became the norm in the U.S., C-sections became routine,[1] accounting for 33% of deliveries in 2008.[29]
We're not advocating for a return to pre-surgery days. C-sections are still saving lives, but according to the WHO, optimal outcomes for moms and babies occur when Cesarean rates are 5-10% of all births. So, yes, some babies *should* make their grand entrance via C-section! If your baby is in a funky position and just won't budge, or one of you is in distress, it may be time to thank modern medicine for the gift of a quick exit.

But if only 5-10% really *need* a section, why are one third of U.S. moms going under the knife? Many assume that today's career-driven mothers are electing surgery to control the calendar. That's a myth. In Childbirth Connection's 2006 "Listening to Mothers II" survey,[30] only 1 in 1600 U.S. mothers asked for a C-section. However, 1 in 4 respondents who had a C-section felt pressured by their health care professional to do so.

---

[1] In the U.S., C-section rates rose 53% from 1996-2007; In Australia, rates rose by 50% from 1997-2007.

Continuous Monitoring

By Nancy Wainer, author of Silent Knife: Cesarean Prevention and Vaginal Birth after Cesarean (VBAC)

Since the advent of continuous monitoring, the C-section rate has skyrocketed without any improvement in maternal or infant outcomes. It turns out, monitors actually do little to nothing to improve maternity care. In addition to other concerns and consequences, they restrict the woman's movement, making it difficult for her to assume positions that would help dilation of the cervix and descent of the baby—and the ever-popular cascade of interventions that lead to preventable Cesarean sections begins.

Intravenous lines with Pitocin are inserted, resulting in drugs and/or epidurals to ward off the unnaturally violent contractions that result. Babies often go into fetal distress, partially as a result of maternal distress and partially due to a number of other factors. And then, because of this kind of "management" of labor…off to the OR they go!

Many years ago, research determined that far too often, Cesareans were being performed for babies who were supposedly distressed—according to the monitors—when in fact, the babies were perfectly fine and there had been no legitimate reason to section those mothers.

"Continuous monitoring" does not have to mean only a machine-operated process. What if the continuous monitor was a person—a loving, calm, skilled, experienced **person** who was with the laboring woman, breathing with her, talking to her, being quiet with her, supporting her. Perhaps what we really need is to monitor our own fears about labor and birth—and keep the machines and the technology at bay. The monitors themselves were not designed for routine use. They were designed for the high-risk situations. But nowadays **everyone** is considered high risk.

You're too old, too young, too fat, too thin, too past your "due" date to have a baby. You are carrying a baby who is too big, too small, with not enough or too much fluid—according to ultrasounds, which are not accurate or safe, either.

I did some of my midwifery training in a very poor country where there were no fetal monitors. No monitors, I thought? How ever would we know HOW the baby was?

And then, over time, I learned that there are many ways to check on the baby during labor without machinery. And I learned that because these mothers did not have Pitocin and epidurals and drugs, the babies were generally quite well, thank you.

At the moment of birth, they breathed. They turned pink. They looked around. They looked for their mommies and they nursed—yes, without all the drugs and machines and technology and making-the-labors-go-faster, they were inherently better off.

The high C-section rate in the U.S. is driven by providers, not patients. Here's why:[31]

Help! I need somebody. Health care providers don't offer continuous labor support, which would boost women's confidence about their birthing ability.

Intervention connection. Common interventions (like inducing first-time moms in non-emergency situations, continuous electronic fetal monitoring, and epidurals given early in labor) often lead to more interventions, which can spiral into C-sections.[32]

She sues me, she sues me not. Doctors may fear malpractice claims, even when a vaginal birth constitutes optimal care.

Bottom first. Obstetricians often opt out of delivering breech babies or presenting a vaginal birth as an option to moms. Giving birth to a breech baby can require more effort from mom and birth provider. A C-section is much more time efficient.[33]

No big deal. U.S. medical professionals, insurance companies, and the public at large carry a casual attitude about surgery and C-sections especially. A quick stitch can fix everything, right?

Cash is king. Providers earn more for performing surgeries than they do when attending vaginal deliveries.

Taboo. Discussing drawbacks isn't common, and health-care providers often downplay the side effects.

Risky Business

A 2006 study found the following risks from C-sections:[34]

Baby beware. Babies are more likely to have surgical cuts, breathing and breastfeeding issues, and asthma.

*Short term...*Moms have more risks of infection, surgical injury, emergency hysterectomy, blood clots, intense and longer-lasting pain, returning to the hospital, and poor overall functioning.

...Long term. Mothers are more likely to have ongoing pelvic pain or bowel blockage, to be injured during future surgeries, and to suffer from infertility. In later pregnancies, mothers are more likely to have an ectopic pregnancy, placenta previa and accreta, placental abruption, and uterine rupture. In other words, your uterus takes a beating.

Once a Section, Always a Section

In the not too distant past, doctors didn't allow a vaginal birth to follow a C-section due to fears of uterine rupture at the prior cut's scar site. These days, OBs are making cuts in spots that are less likely to rupture in later deliveries. As research grows, Vaginal Birth After Cesarean (VBAC), a term coined by Nancy Wainer, is proving safer than we once thought.[35] Hospitals are also becoming more transparent: they're posting their VBAC stats to give a better understanding of how supportive their staff is, should a birthing mom want to go that route. Due to medical issues or other circumstances, some women will need to undergo another C-section. Others don't have the facts or support to make an informed decision.

WHEN "WHAT IF?" BECOMES "WHAT DID"

You've seen the numbers. Most Western moms give birth in the hospital. Of those, most experience some sort of intervention, and one in three has a C-section. So there's a high likelihood of not birthing as hoped.

After a disappointing or traumatic birth, moms may experience postpartum depression, anxiety and even PTSD. Thankfully, support groups abound. Whether online or in person, reach out and start healing. Once you've emotionally processed your birth experience, you'll free up energy to mother your precious little one.

The numbers paint a clear picture: nine out of ten moms who've had a C-section schedule another one for their next birth.[36]

If you've had surgery and want additional support, check out the International Cesarean Awareness Network (ICAN). It seeks to prevent unnecessary Cesareans by providing support and information.

Prevention, Midwife Style

In general, midwives view C-sections as largely over-performed to solve "pseudo-problems."[37] Nancy Wainer, who has attended over 1,600 births, says one of the most effective and least implemented strategies for better birthing is baby positioning. Instead of performing major surgery, a simple shift of baby's pose could move labor forward. While prevention is key to keeping baby from misalignment—(see "Priming to Push" for tips)—a skilled midwife may save you from a long surgical recovery, using extensive preventative care during early labor and suggestions during the transition and pushing phases.

Welcome, Baby!

Ready for some *other* ways to usher in the first hours of life? If you're delivering in a hospital and plan to implement alternative practices, make sure your partner and doctor are on the same page by discussing your preferences early and often. Be prepared for some raised eyebrows from the establishment. First-time moms who subvert the system are pretty rare.

Cutting Ties

The umbilical cord is literally a lifeline. It connects mom to baby, and baby to his source of nourishment in the womb. So why the rush to clamp it? A review of cord clamping studies from 1980 to 2001 concluded, "Immediate clamping of the umbilical cord can reduce the red blood cells an infant receives at birth by more than 50%, resulting in potential short-term and long-term neonatal problems."[38]

Early cord clamping can be even more serious if you're anemic. A study of babies born to anemic mothers found "the risk for anemia at three months of age was almost eight times higher in the early clamping group compared to the delayed clamping group."[39] In infants whose cord clamping was delayed until the blood flow stopped, "higher red blood cell flow to vital organs in the first week was noted, and term infants had less anemia at two months and increased duration of early nursing."[40]

Homebirth midwives generally wait to cut the cord until it stops pulsing, but most hospitals cut it almost immediately.

It's helpful to know that some doctors inject Pitocin immediately after they deliver the shoulders, as there's some evidence that this may reduce postpartum hemorrhaging in at-risk mothers.[41] If you're thinking of opting out, let your provider know ahead of time. The cord has to be cut immediately if you do get this late-dose Pitocin, to ensure your baby doesn't absorb the drug.

Skin-to-Skin

We can't rave enough about the benefits of skin-to-skin contact immediately after birth (and beyond!). As a baby transitions from the womb to the world, mom can mimic his prior home by offering him the warmth and security of her touch.

When a baby is placed on his mother's chest, (or dad's if mom is unable) his temperature, heart rate, blood pressure and blood sugar regulate. Skin-to-skin contact also improves breastfeeding success rates in the short and long term,[42] and helps colonization of the baby's skin with his mother's 'good' bacteria, improving his immunity and reducing his likelihood of developing allergies![43]

Some staffers whisk the baby away for cleaning, measurements, or testing before mom speaks up. So, if you want to keep your baby close for the first hour, share your plans with the staff—explicitly and confidently—beforehand.

In addition to the physical benefits of skin-to-skin contact, a newborn feels more secure and cries less, and therefore doesn't release the stress hormone, cortisol, into the bloodstream.[44] Crying newborns also release somastostatin in their guts, which decreases absorption of food and inhibits growth. Research has found babies who've had significant skin-to-skin time have brains better wired for development, stay warmer, cry less[45] and enjoy more peaceful cycles of sleep.[46]

Hold that Bath!

Immediately after birth, nurses run a quick bath to wash blood and vernix off the baby. But wait! While it's a good idea to remove the blood, a simple wipe with a dry cloth is sufficient. Vernix is actually incredibly healing. It's not only moisturizing, which helps with postpartum peeling, but also antimicrobial, which protects against the possibility of infection.

Aside from removing vernix, baths can unsafely lower a newborn's body temperature, and interrupt mother-baby bonding time.[47] Studies found that removing vernix through early bathing leaves babies vulnerable to group B streptococcus and E. coli.[48]

If you choose to skip the bath, don't be offended if there's a sign on your little one's bassinet telling the world he's unbathed. It's standard hospital procedure for staff to wear gloves when touching unbathed babies because hospitals consider them biohazards!

Forget Your Vitamins

Back when mamas were heavily sedated throughout labor and delivery, babies were often pulled through the birth canal with forceps (knocked out mamas can't push!). Not surprisingly, newborns had some pretty significant bruises from their traumatic delivery. Immediate cord cutting meant that beneficial stem cells, and up to 50% of the baby's blood volume, complete with natural clotting factors, were shut down. As fewer moms breastfed, babies lost access to vitamin K-rich colostrum. Add it up, and we have a clotting problem on our hands.[49]

If a baby's blood doesn't clot, he may experience a rare form of brain hemorrhaging, known as vitamin K deficiency bleeding (VKDB). The disease affects 0.25%-1.7% of babies in their first week of life, and almost all cases involve an early cord clamp or a traumatic birth.[50] A second form of the disease affects .004-.007% of two-to-twelve week old babies. These newborns have breastfeeding moms with a massive vitamin K deficiency or liver trauma due to alcohol consumption during pregnancy. Recreational drugs, epilepsy or tuberculosis medicines and anticoagulants are also risk factors.[51]

Savvy doctors found a way to counter the issue. They manufactured a synthetic, injectable form of Vitamin K at 20,000 times the natural level, to promote adequate blood clotting. These shots are given to newborns as standard practice in U.S. hospitals. Oral Vitamin K doses are available in Europe and Asia, and have shown similar results to the shot, although they are administered in several doses.

If you skip the Vitamin K shot, both you and your midwife or OB should be vigilant in looking for excessive bruising, or bleeding from umbilical cord, eyes, or nose. In those situations, an immediate dose could save a baby's life.

Nature usually gets these things right, though. If left alone, our levels rise gradually, naturally, as they have for millennia. Perhaps the healthier solution is a return to natural, gentle birthing, complete with a skilled birth attendant and plenty of breastfeeding support.

Megan, A Novel Mama

The Choice is Yours

At the last La Leche League meeting I attended while pregnant, Jaime's words stuck in my mind: "Everything is optional." I didn't have to send my baby to the nursery; I didn't have to let the nurses take her to another room to get weighed, or have her vision checked. Everything could be done in our room.

Optional, yes. Easy? No. But while I recovered post delivery, though my nipples were raw and my eyelids heavy, I held those words dear. When nurses asked to take Anabella, I responded politely—and firmly—that my newborn didn't need to be weighed in a cold, hard scale a hundred yards away. I heard hushed whispers. The night staff didn't know what to make of me.

State law mandated Anabella get her blood drawn before discharge. But anything that could happen in a nursery could happen in my room. So the nurse brought a needle, paperwork, and some incredulity. She drew blood while Anabella nursed peacefully. The nurse said it was the easiest draw she'd done.

These days, power isn't often served on a silver platter. But it is ours for the taking, if we know our rights.

Eyes Wide Open

If you give birth at a hospital and nurses take your baby to weigh and clean, they also apply eye drops. This procedure began because bacteria in birth canals of women with gonorrhea or Chlamydia caused blindness in infants.

Two types of medication are used in eye drops: erythromycin or silver nitrate. Silver nitrate, though less widely used, is a proven eye irritant that creates a burning sensation. Even if your baby gets erythromycin, it can make his vision blurry.[52]

Although some states mandate the drops, you can request they be delayed until after breastfeeding, or whenever you feel appropriate. Wondering how your newborn will see the world with gunk in his baby blues? Grab a tube of erythromycin on your hospital tour and put it in your eyes promptly upon waking.

The Circumcision Decision

If you have a baby boy, chances are you'll be asked whether or not you want to circumcise him in the hospital. Most of us have inherited a vague sense that circumcision is somehow cleaner or healthier. But these are myths. We'll share a few facts to jumpstart your research.

- The significance of the infant's pain is often overlooked in circumcision. Hospitals use painful Gomco clamps that sever nerve endings,[53] and most docs make the cut without anesthesia.
- Many infants go into shock as a result of the pain they experience in circumcision, and the breastfeeding relationship may be compromised as a result.
- The circumcised penis is no cleaner than an intact penis, and requires far more care during the healing process.
- "...[P]rofessional societies representing Australian, Canadian, and American pediatricians do not recommend routine circumcision of male newborns."[54] ~American Medical Association

What if you plan to circumcise for reasons of Jewish faith? In Jewish circumcisions,

- Boys are circumcised eight days after birth, when natural levels of Vitamin K are the highest.
- Anesthetic is traditionally given (in the form of a tiny amount of wine and/or numbing agents).
- Mohels (traditional circumcisers) don't use painful skin clamps.

Overheard...

After reading up on circumcision, I knew I didn't want to go through with it. The first reason was medical: the AAP doesn't recommend routine circumcision. My second reason was emotional. It went against my mama bear instinct to protect my baby.

Convincing dad was more difficult. He wanted to have his son like him. (I asked him if he and his dad compared their penises; the answer was no.) My husband watched videos of the procedure being done but had to stop them before they were over.

He'd thought it was a simple snip of the 'extra' skin, but it's not. The foreskin is actually fused to the head of the penis, like a fingernail to a nail bed. We took our baby home from the hospital the way he was born, and we haven't regretted it.

~Lani, mom to Bentley

Want to learn more? Check out the Circumcision Resource Center online, a helpful resource filled with medical and psychological literature for those questioning the practice.

To Vax or Not to Vax?

The vaccine debate is heated, and those who tread the middle ground must sort through data, holes in data, and emotionally-charged claims of both sides. Pro and anti-vax camps claim serious or deadly consequences if their path isn't followed. While alarmists ring bells on both sides, it's our goal to support you by being a catalyst for careful independent thought.

Please hear us clearly: we are neither endorsing nor condemning vaccines. We're sharing information that is grounded in credible science and has been approved by both our consciences (one of us chose to vaccinate fully, and the other to forgo completely). Your decision to vaccinate is highly personal. It may begin with research, but is ultimately a product of your philosophy of health and wellness, and perception of the risks.

Infant Vaccines Today

Vaccines are now standard procedure: all 50 of the United States require students to be vaccinated before they enroll in school. But religious, medical and often philosophical exemptions are granted. Vaccines were touted as the 20th century's best medical breakthrough, but skepticism is on the rise.

Some parents opt to skip shots altogether because of questionable ingredients and reported links to illnesses. Others delay vaccines for months or years, because they're concerned about injecting their baby's immune system with viruses and foreign substances. Some families space out vaccinations in a way that seems more manageable. But most parents proceed with the standard schedule.

Theoretically Speaking...

Vaccines are designed to help us develop immunities against illnesses by injecting a killed or weakened germ into our systems. The germ is weak enough not to infect a baby with the illness, but stimulates his immune system to develop antibodies that protect him against the virus. In theory, these antibodies should defend the baby's system from exposure to the actual illness.

Herd Immunity

Vaccines have become a public health mandate in order to protect populations, not just individuals. While not every vaccinated individual develops immunity, when enough individuals respond to a vaccine, the disease pathogen won't be able to survive, limiting or eliminating the chances of outbreak.

Vaccine proponents urge all parents to vaccinate their children in order to protect both immune and non-immune people, because if non-immune persons fall below about 70%-90% (depending on the disease), epidemics can break out. Mass vaccination does not exclusively benefit the individual, or else some wouldn't be so bothered about others' refusal: it also protects an entire population.

Overheard...

When I was a Girl Scout growing up in Mexico City, we visited a home for kids suffering from Polio. They were not vaccinated against it as infants, and it left a lasting impression. I followed the traditional schedule of vaccines, just like my doctor did with her four kids. In my opinion, the risks of not vaccinating far outweigh the risks of vaccinating.

~Andrea, mom to Mateo and Stefan

Track Record

Though there are naysayers on even this point, vaccines have several successes under their belt: smallpox and tetanus, to start. Yet, the mortality rates from some of the biggest childhood killers had dropped quite low even before the introduction of vaccines. While diphtheria once killed 5 of every 1,000 children, when its vaccine was approved, mortality had reached an all-time low of 6 per 100,000.[55] In less than a century, the death rate from measles dropped from 13% to less than 1 in 100,000—before the vaccine was introduced in 1963.[56] Sweden dropped the pertussis vaccine in 1979 because 84% of 5,140 infected cases had been vaccinated at least three times.[57]

Murky Ingredients

Mercury. If you're aware of the vaccine debate, you've likely heard concerns that mercury may be linked to autism. The ingredient in question was thimerosal, a preservative that contains mercury, which is used in some vaccines. The CDC claims it's harmless, aside from minor redness or swelling at the site of the shot. When an advisory committee determined that ethylmercury was unsafe in 1980, manufacturers were urged to reduce thimerosal in vaccines as a "precautionary measure." The measure didn't go into effect until 1998. Most vaccines are now mercury-free. But bring this up for a reason: if a neurotoxin was allowed in vaccines for decades, what else is in there?

> **Overheard...**
>
> *Before having children, I worked with a man whose son had mercury poisoning as a toddler, and was later diagnosed with Autism. As I started researching, I realized many children have been injured from vaccines. Because I believe in alternative treatments like homeopathy, I decided I'd take the risk of my kids contracting a disease, rather than inject potentially toxic vaccines into their developing immune systems.*
>
> *I understand that ours is a privileged position. I imagine that if I were traveling in the developing world, I might consider selectively vaccinating.*
>
> *~Diana, mom to Shama and Leela*

Aluminum. Another concerning ingredient is aluminum, which is used in vaccines as a preservative. If you follow the recommended vaccine schedule, you're likely to inject 10 to 50 times the safe dose of aluminum set by the FDA in a given doctor's visit.[58] Excessive levels have been shown to permanently damage the brain and kidneys.[59]

Ick. Some other troubling ingredients in vaccines: human albumin (blood proteins), chicken embryo protein, monkey kidney cells, formaldehyde, cow fetus serum, and more. Transparency in vaccines keeps big pharma accountable, and empowers parents to make informed decisions. But we have a long way to go before manufacturers and doctors are forthright with *all* the facts, not just the ones that present well.

The Cost of Doing Business

The U.S. National Vaccine Injury Compensation Program (VICP) was created in 1988 to compensate for injuries and deaths induced by vaccines, many of which didn't contain mercury. Ironically, manufacturers aren't funding this pool; taxpayers are. The VICP has paid more than $2 billion in claims since its inception.

The Big Picture

When we look at health outcomes for infants who've been vaccinated, compared with those who have not, a majority of the data shows that individual and public health outcomes improve with vaccines.[60] So, doctors work to ensure that infants get the recommended shots, on schedule. We believe they're well intentioned, but they don't take into account individual circumstances or concerns.

It's your job to know your child, weigh the risks of disease exposure against the risk of vaccine injury, and make your own best decision. You can do your part too—the first line of defense against illness is breastfeeding.

Taking Precautions

If you decide to vaccinate, there are a number of steps you can take to make sure your baby is as safe as can be.

- Research each vaccine separately.
- Make sure your child is 100% healthy. Injecting a foreign substance into your blood shocks the immune system. If a baby is fighting a cold or illness, it can overtax his system.[61]
- Give your baby therapeutic doses of Vitamin C[62] for a week before and two weeks after each shot.

- Ask a licensed homeopath about remedies that can safely be taken with vaccines to reverse or lessen injection side effects.
- Dr. Janet Zand recommends putting 1-2 drops of Bach's Rescue Remedy under your baby's tongue after the shot to alleviate the emotional stress of the injection.[63]
- On the day of the shot, check your doctor's vaccine batch against the VAERS database. If any red flags have been reported, you'll be in the know, and can make an informed decision.
- Ask your pedi if shots can be given over several visits. Each doctor has a preferred shot schedule, but some parents feel more comfortable giving just one shot per visit.

Go Gently

The first days of your baby's life are a magical and terrifying time—for both of you! Whether you birthed your baby at home, or brought him back to your pad after his big debut, the name of the game is Change. Your newborn will be getting used to sights, sounds, and smells. You will be adjusting to less sleep, a rebounding body, and most importantly, a new role. Now is the time to be gentle with yourself.

Whether you had a two-hour delivery or a forty-eight hour labor ending in a C-section, you've been through a lot. It helps enormously to accept all offers of food, cleaning, and childcare for older siblings!

Overheard...

The first days at home felt otherworldly—I was consumed by this tiny being. I forgot everything else; I couldn't sleep if she wasn't right with me; I couldn't eat until she had eaten and was content. I needed my mom and my husband to care for me because I was so wrapped up in my little tiny girl. The first time I left the house, I was shocked that the world was still the same as it had been before, when I felt so different.

~Melissa, mom to Elena

Under the Sheets

Sex brought that precious new being into your life. And yet for many, the baby takes sex out of your life, at least for the short term. According to one study, 90% of couples resume intercourse by six months postpartum.[64] For some mamas, especially those who have delivered naturally and been struck by the awesomeness of their birthing body, sex is even better than before. For other women, especially moms who had a disappointing birth experience, returning to physical intimacy with their partners can be a slow process.

Postpartum emotions figure into your libido too. You may feel exhilarated, exhausted, in love, irritable, or all of the above. Chemistry is at play here too—hormones like estrogen, progesterone, and oxytocin are surging and dropping as your body adjusts to its postpartum state. It's no wonder some new mothers get more excited about a solo nap than a romp in the bedroom.

No matter where you are on the spectrum, it's helpful to remember that birthing a baby is physically intense. (As if some of us could forget!) The tender, delicate tissues and muscles of your vagina works in synchronicity, stretching, caressing baby, and sometimes tearing, in order to complete its greatest accomplishment: bringing forth life. You were made for this! Your body knows just how long it needs to recover, so forget statistics, mom forums and prior births.

Every birth requires its own unique path to healing. That's not a popular sentiment, though. Most OBs and midwives will likely advise waiting until your six-week postpartum visit before restarting your sex life. There's no science behind that number, and quite frankly, no one should be putting time limits on another's body.

If you do wait for the "official" go-ahead, don't expect a crash course in postpartum sex. When a provider gives a green light, they often stop there. Some women are unprepared for their first after-baby experience. There is normally less estrogen in your body during breastfeeding, and since estrogen is responsible for mucus production, moms may find their lady parts dry. In addition to dryness, vaginal walls thin out, which can be painful with friction. A good lube works wonders, though. Coconut oil and olive oil are natural options that provide healing benefits.

Everything Changes

Even if you're technically functioning fine, you may or may not feel super sexy. We've heard of women who go to the grocery store the day after their birth in pre-pregnancy jeans, but most of us take longer to shed the baby weight. And when we do, things have usually shifted. Breastfeeding, eating a healthy diet, and exercising will speed up the process, but give yourself a break. It took almost a year to make that beautiful baby, so you're entitled to at least that much time to recoup. And we'll be honest—for some moms, things may never be the same. Instead of lamenting the loss of your pre-baby body, wear your birth proudly. You are now a mother.

Other physical conditions that lead to that less-than-sexy feeling are lack of sleep, the emotional stresses of being a new mom (no matter how much you love your baby!), and bodily fatigue from blood loss. To combat the blood loss, beef up on iron in the form of red meat, leafy greens, or legumes in the weeks after childbirth.

While rocky emotions are not abnormal for a few days, if sad and anxious feelings continue past the third week, call your provider. True postpartum depression (PPD) affects 10-20% of all birthing moms and up to 50% of high-risk mamas.[65] Good news: you can be treated! Visit your health care provider to find out your options. If left untreated, PPD can profoundly impact your relationship with your baby and partner, and your wellbeing.

These complex factors all play into your sexual desire. If friends and family gave you a reprieve from household responsibilities, and you rocked that birth, you may find it easier to bounce back. Moms who must immediately take up their day-to-day tasks generally have a longer, slower recuperation. Talking with your partner about your desire (or lack thereof), and the contributing factors, is key. Keeping communication open, even though neither of you can fully understand what the other is going through, fosters emotional intimacy rather than distance. Emotional support and a sense of closeness are what every new mom needs!

Overheard...

After my C-section, it took about four months before we got back to "normal." After my VBAC, it took more like six months, as everything seemed...different.

Of course it never really gets back to normal with kids around. No more lazy Sunday mornings cuddling in bed or long, romantic dinners. For us, humor and a sense of fun have had to make up for sporadic at best romance, but I think we're stronger for it.

~Courtney, mom to Mack and Liam

In Good Company

Some women talk to anyone and everyone about sex. Others are more private and prefer to find answers on the Internet or discuss with a trusted friend. No matter where you fall on the spectrum, hearing from other moms helps to normalize your experience.

Overheard…

We had sex 17 days after my homebirth. If it weren't for the vaginal soreness, I probably would have acted that night! It was my first baby, and I labored for 17 1/2 hours. I felt beautiful, strong, capable… different. I felt so much better, like I had walked out of some war, and I had survived by my own will. And the way my husband looked at me like he thought I was amazing—it was enough to make my mind ready long before my body.

~Titus, mom to Angelle

Our midwife announced—in front of my husband—that we needed to wait six weeks before having sex again, and my husband started his stopwatch when we left the appointment. My body, however, did NOT agree with the brief reprieve and took 8 months to be able to have sex. It was frustrating for both of us.

I wish we had both been told that it can take a lot longer for some couples to get back to normal.

~Colette, mom to Millie and Sammy

I expected that my libido would be diminished for quite a while after our son arrived. While it's true that in the initial month I had no energy for sex, I did find that, surprisingly, my desire for my husband actually increased post-baby.

The experience of child-raising has deepened our intimacy considerably—and the sex has been great!! I never expected that "side effect" of giving birth!

~Rachel, mom to Sean

Your Best Birth

What a ride! Anyone who's witnessed the arrival of a new life leaves with an intense appreciation for the power of women. Growing, birthing, and easing into motherhood requires a new level of strength—one we often didn't know we had. Moms are biologically predisposed to selective forgetfulness, and ultimately, a newly expanded heart and precious new addition help blur the memory of earlier trials.

Birth is one of the most amazing, intense, humbling experiences you'll ever go through. Even if your birth doesn't go as planned, educating yourself enables you to participate from a place of strength, rather than fear.

Touch
nurture with affection

Imagine you've just come into the world. It's bright, noisy, and completely different from the womb. You're hearing and seeing and feeling strange new sensations. After 40 weeks of constant closeness, warmth, and security, everything is suddenly different and overwhelming. As newbies to the outside world, infants crave a return to womb-like sensations. And the most important of those is touch.

Touching grounds us. If we're unraveling, having a trusted friend take our hand can help center us. Touching is the sense that connects us with others in a tangible way. Touch mimics our formative experience in the womb. It's the only one of our five senses that none of us is born without.

The importance of being in physical contact with our babies has been known for centuries, and is being rediscovered today. In this chapter we'll decode our culture's lingering beliefs about spoiling babies with too much handling. We'll share the science behind the magic of touch, and how to safely stay close to your baby using our favorite accessory—the baby carrier.

The Demonization of Touch

Across time and oceans, touch has been used by mothers as a simple and effective way to nurture their babies.

Yet, after the industrial revolution, 18th century child-rearing literature throughout the Western world began reflecting now-familiar fears of "spoiling" babies through physical touch and soothing.

During the 1800s, more than half of American-born infants died before their first birthday, due to a disease called marasmus, or "wasting away," also known as infant atrophy. As the movement against "spoiling" babies through touch picked up speed, in the 1920s almost 100% of institutionalized infants died before their first birthday. What are the implications? Without touch, babies were literally left to waste away. Sounds like the very definition of spoiling.

Overheard...

My doctor told me you couldn't spoil an infant, so I was reassured I could do what comes naturally—hold my baby all the time, nurse him whenever he needed it, and give him all the love he deserves.

~Shannon, mom to Kai

Attachment Theory and Touch

Your baby is so happy! It's amazing how he makes eye contact and smiles directly at you! Mamas who are hands on—literally—hear these comments all the time. And research validates what, to many mothers, is common sense: the more you hold your baby, the happier and more engaged he is.[1]

What we're talking about is a healthy attachment. In layman's terms, this is a baby's confidence that his mom is striving to meet his needs. He is assured that he has an advocate, caregiver, and source of comfort, day in and day out. We've woven the theme of attachment throughout *The Other Baby Book*, both explicitly and implicitly, because it underlies all we do as nurturing mamas.

We'll explore the subject in a bit more depth now though, because we're up against an entrenched "don't spoil the baby" cultural legacy. And the more we can arm you with research to verify what we know in our hearts to be true—babies need our loving touch—the more confident you can be when disregarding the well-intentioned but harmful comments of strangers, family and even friends.

A baby's secure attachment to his primary caregiver lays the foundation for a lifetime of healthy self-esteem and strong relationships with others. Your relationship will carry him through his whole life, and will be reflected in how he views himself and others. As if that weren't enough, a recent study found that early nurturing impacts brain size![2] School-aged children whose parents nurtured them in their first years had a larger hippocampus, the part of the brain responsible for memory, learning and stress response.

The intensive first year together is also when mom learns how to mother in general, and how to parent this baby in particular. Mothers get to know her little one's needs and quirks, and how best to hold, comfort and nurture him. Early memories of loving touch establish a mother as her baby's safe haven into his childhood years and beyond, and confirm his inherent value and lovability.

Overheard...

People constantly remark how happy, smiley, and engaging our son is. From five weeks, he'd initiate eye contact with people and smile or interact with them. Others found him much more interactive than was expected for his age. He was held most of the time in our arms or in a carrier, including when he napped, and we did massage and other forms of nurturing touch.

~Heidi, mom to Sam

The First Hours of Life

Labor of Love

As your baby exits the warm embrace and constant motion of the womb, the physical stimulation of labor helps his body wake up to the world. Humans are the only mammals who don't lick their young immediately following birth, an action that energizes the skin and body of the newborn. Instead, the ride through the birth canal stimulates the baby's skin as he emerges. This vigorous massage is an introduction to a physical world where mothers' instincts, when nurtured, ensure nearly continuous touch and care.

Early and Often

Babies used to be taken to nurseries to sit in a well-heated plastic box for the first twelve hours or so. The good news is that most hospitals got the memo about the benefits of early mother-baby bonding, especially the all-important skin-to-skin contact we discussed in Birth. In fact, moms who are given the chance to bond in the first 30 minutes after birth show significantly more attachment behaviors in the months following birth, compared to those pairs who were separated during the first few minutes.[3]

Overheard...

After the intensity of giving birth, holding my baby naked on my chest right after his birth was a truly calm and peaceful moment. It was like we were completely alone, and the sounds around us were barely real.

~Sarah, mom to William

Home is Where the Heart is

Most mothers cradle their babies on the left.[4] Though mama may not be cognizant of it at the time, the baby hears her heartbeat better on that side. Research supports moms' intuition.[5] Babies in a hospital nursery who were exposed to the sound of heartbeats gained more weight than babies who didn't. Also, the left side of the body corresponds to the right brain, which is skilled at processing emotions and more equipped to build a bond with baby than the analytical left brain. And on a practical final note, most moms are right-handed, so when holding the baby with her left hand she can use her right hand to access what she needs.

A Milky Embrace

As we'll discuss in the next chapter, babies process human milk quickly, making frequent feedings necessary for survival. Not only is the nutritional content of the milk crucial for development, but the warmth and comfort of being held in arms and nursed is deeply nurturing to the baby's sense of security. Babies reap benefits from a cuddly bottle feed too, though! In a famous experiment, researcher Harry Harlow found that baby monkeys clung to a wire "mother" stand-in with a bit of soft cloth rather than a wire "mother" with milk. The bottom line? Warm touch is more desired than life-giving milk (after feeding needs have been met, of course). When a baby is secure, his biological development continues at an ideal pace.

Put that Baby Down!

Thanks to our cultural legacy of withholding affection, many moms today are afraid if they hold their baby too much, he'll get used to it and become increasingly demanding. (Studies have consistently shown the opposite, but we'll get to that later.) Duly cautioned, modern moms make sure to put the baby down often and in different apparatuses, like baby swings, bouncy seats, strollers, bassinets and cribs. One of the most pervasive practices is supporting solo sleep. In our quest to raise independent children and protect the sanctity of the marital bed, many of us don't question the value of putting babies to sleep on their own as soon as possible.

Anna Freud, the founder of child psychoanalysis, cautions in her book, *Normality and Pathology in Childhood,*[6]

> *It is a primitive need of the child to have close and warm contact with another person's body while falling asleep, but this runs counter to all the rules of hygiene which demand that children sleep by themselves and not share the parental bed. ...As a result, mothers seek advice for infants who have difficulty in falling asleep or do not sleep through the night, in spite of being tired.*

Fit to be Touched

Touch is important, but not just for a baby to feel loved. It's actually crucial to the successful growth and development of babies in the first months and years of life. In a series of interesting experiments with baby rats (or "pups" as they are technically called), one group was caressed and cuddled by its human caretaker, and the other group was treated coldly. The group of pups that was petted learned and grew faster than their lonely counterparts.[7] Similar studies were done on pregnant rats, with similar outcomes on the pups, showing that pampering the mama is important for her baby's health, too! Massage in preterm infants has been associated with greater and faster weight gain than their non-massaged counterparts.[8]

Early touch is important to help babies establish a foundation of positive emotions for later infancy, which carries forward into childhood and adulthood. Babies whose mothers failed to touch them sufficiently between one week and three months displayed signs of anger and aggression between nine and twelve months of age.[9] On the flip side, a baby who has been sufficiently loved develops a secure attachment to mom, making his first year special for the whole family.

But before we go overboard, it's important to note that new babies are extremely sensitive to touch and for some, being touched can cause stress. Fortunately for parents, your little one is an open book.

Midwife and Early Attachment Specialist Karina Dyer gave us some tips for reading a baby's cues. If he's in the mood for more, he'll make eye contact, engage you through vocalizations, or be relaxed and still, turning toward you. But if he's not ready to pass Go, he may use various behaviors to put an end to the stimulation. These cues include turning away, putting a hand to his mouth, yawning, spitting up, hiccupping, closing his eyes, becoming physically tense or floppy, arching his back and eventually crying.

Of course, your baby may put his hand to his mouth because he's teething, or yawn because he's tired. Keying in to your baby's signs takes careful observation. Dyer notes,

> Touch is a very intimate form of communication and just as we would with another adult, we must take the time to gain 'permission' to touch. This shows a baby he is respected, and teaches him that his needs are important and understood.[10]

The Crying Game: Emotional Effects of Touch

If you've spent more than a few hours with a newborn, there's one thing you know: they cry. Some cry a lot, especially during the first few months. And the more they are left to cry, the more they do. A baby cries to communicate his needs. An infant who is calmed quickly and regularly learns to trust his caregivers, and can afford to give a little more slack in the future.

But when caregivers don't respond, the baby is more likely to quickly escalate his cries to get more attention. (Though eventually, babies learn to stop when their cries are repeatedly ignored.) These are survival instincts at work. He's crying because he needs to be fed, held, warmed, changed, etc., and mom, especially after a grueling birth, may need a reminder. The more in sync mama is, the more a baby's emergency system can relax a bit, since survival is less of a concern when he knows help is at his fingertips.

Crying can be frightening, frustrating, irritating, and just plain crazy-making. And that's just for the caretaker. So what kind of impact does crying have on babies? Hint: it's even worse. Because their systems are so fragile and still developing, crying takes up an unhealthy amount of internal resources. The good news? In addition to providing frequent access to the breast, touch is a mutually enjoyable way to soothe your baby's tears.

Crying is both a symptom and trigger of stress. As we mentioned in Birth, excessive crying increases both stress hormones and blood flow to the brain. Too many tears also slow that blood from draining from the brain, which can be dangerous.[11] Consistently slow responses to babies' cries increases sensitivity to stress in adulthood and may lead to post-traumatic stress and panic disorders in adulthood, according to researchers at Harvard Medical School's Department of Psychiatry. Kids who excessively cry in infancy have lower IQ scores.[12]

While this is a point of contention among researchers, mothers, and baby experts, it's possible sometimes babies just need to cry as a way of releasing tension and aiding relaxation, often at the end of a busy day, and mom isn't able to stop it. But perhaps stopping it shouldn't be the main goal. Instead of going through a laundry list of ways to get her baby to *just be quiet*, mom can 'be with' her baby during the distress, showing him that even though she can't make things better, she's there to support him, and isn't afraid of her baby's strong emotions. This support acts as a brick in the foundation that a child will use to process and manage his future emotions.

Touch that Colic Away

Colic, a condition in which a baby cries often and for extended periods of time, is one of new parents' greatest fears in Western society. Our societies like to talk about these "fussy babies" as if they're different from other babies. Interestingly, in some societies, colic is unheard of.[13]

Megan, A Novel Mama

Defying Statistics

A purple, organic Moby wrap (baby carrier) was my mainstay for the first three months of Anabella's life. Even in her saddest, colicky moments, Anabella was calmeest on my chest, hugged tight by the Moby.

I admit—I was surprised. I'd read so many studies on the benefits of holding your baby close, and thought babywearing equaled a ticket to a colic-free infancy. Despite these research outcomes, there were moments when the tail of my wrap dragged behind me, and Anabella's cries rang in my ears. It didn't mean I wasn't touching, loving or nursing her enough. It meant we were both human.

Sometimes I woke up on the wrong side of the bed, or just needed a good cry, so I allowed my girl the same freedom. Those trying times were when I prayed the hardest, and saw the bottom of the ice cream carton. But at the end of the day, I knew I was doing Anabella right by holding her close and letting her vent in the safety of my arms.

Loving touch, combined with lots of nursing, can significantly reduce your baby's tears.

Moms of colicky babies who were told not to let their babies cry—to pick them up, hold them, feed them on cue, or let their little ones comfort nurse—cried 70% less than a control group of colicky infants, who had no change, and cried 2.5 times more than average infants.[14]

How Touch Shapes Mom

Touch is not only beneficial for babies. As mom gets to know her newborn in the most direct possible way—through physical contact—she also gets to know herself as a mother. Maternal instincts grow through direct interaction with our babies. The more a mom touches her baby, the more she connects to her nurturing instincts.

Does Swaddling Affect Breastfeeding?

By Nancy Mohrbacher, IBCLC, author of Breastfeeding Made Simple: Seven Natural Laws for Nursing Mothers

The effect of swaddling on breastfeeding is especially important in the early weeks, when frequent nursing is key to establishing healthy milk production. Baby's inborn breastfeeding behaviors are triggered by the feel of a baby's front (head, torso, legs, and feet) against mother's body. Have you ever seen the videos of babies crawling to the breast without help? Babies can do that when they are tummy down on mom's body.

This frontal contact with mother triggers these instinctive feeding behaviors even when baby is in a light sleep. One study found that when mothers kept their babies primarily on their bodies during the first day of life, they actively fed for an average of 2.5 hours.

When newborns are swaddled and laid on a separate surface, this body stimulation is missing. Without it, babies may go for much longer stretches without nursing, which can affect milk production, cause newborn jaundice and engorgement in the mother. During the first month of life, frequent feedings are critical to establishing healthy milk production. Keeping babies swaddled for many hours can significantly affect early breastfeeding.

One study of 22,000 mothers and babies found that the longer mothers and babies are in skin-to-skin contact during the first three hours after birth (which swaddling prevents), the more likely they are to be exclusively breastfeeding at hospital discharge.[15] Those babies who spent at least one hour of the first three hours of life in skin-to-skin contact were more than three times more likely to be exclusively breastfeeding at hospital discharge than those who had no skin-to-skin contact during the first three hours.

A meta-analysis published by the Cochrane Review examined 30 studies with 1925 participants and concluded that when full-term, healthy babies received early skin-to-skin contact after birth, "babies interacted more with their mothers, stayed warmer, and cried less. Babies were more likely to be breastfed, and to nurse for longer, if they had early skin-to-skin contact."[16]

Baby carriers enable mom to stay in touch with her baby, promoting secure attachment. In a study comparing infants of mothers who used soft baby carriers to those who used stand-alone infant seats, moms who used carriers were much more responsive at three months than the moms who used seats. At 13 months, far more of the carried babies were securely attached to their mamas than the seated babies.[17]

Swaddling: Under Wraps

Swaddling is used around the world to give babies a feeling of being enclosed, to help create a womb-like environment. The practice offers some benefits of touch, and can be soothing. Most hospitals today teach new families to swaddle. But parents and experts alike are expressing concerns that swaddling is being used instead of touch. We favor the human swaddle—strapping baby to mom, ideally skin-to-skin, to replicate the sensations and benefits of the womb.

Infant Massage

Massage is gaining traction as an essential tool for parent-baby bonding, health, and development. Studies have shown that infants who are massaged reap a variety of health benefits. In moms with postpartum depression, quality of mother-child interaction improved, helping to lay the foundation for a strong relationship. Preemies who were massaged: [18]

- gained 30–50% more weight than non-massaged babies;
- boasted length and head circumference growth increases;
- had greater bone mineral density as a result of massage.

Encouragingly, infant massage classes are becoming increasingly available to new moms. Many communities and hospitals now offer free or low cost massage classes, promoting early bonding between babies and caregivers and improved infant health.

Touching Across Cultures

If physical contact were a competitive sport, the U.S. team would be the consistent loser, year after year. Korean babies are held 90% of time, as compared with 33% of the time for U.S. babies, who spend most of their infancy in car seats, cribs and strollers.[19] Taking into account the many emotional and biological benefits of touch, it's no wonder Americans report record rates of anxiety and depression.

Co-Bathing

We're going to get radical. Would you consider taking the Funtime Froggy bathtub off your registry? We have an alternative that may make you love bath time—and, as a bonus, you'll save some room in the landfills. Rather than the mutually stressful experience of positioning your newborn alone in a plastic tub, how about making his first bath a shared experience? Mothers across the ages and around the world have instinctively dipped into the river, the lake, or the bathtub with their little ones. By bathing with your baby, you soften the impact of what might be a new and frightening experience for him. If he's hungry, he can nurse. If he's cold, your body temperature will keep him toasty. If he's afraid, you're right there with him. And it's fun!

Overheard...

I thought all babies loved bath time. All my friends liked bathing their children to help them relax before bed, so I didn't understand why Dalia cried. As I talked to other moms, I was surprised to learn that one friend got into the tub with her baby. After rejecting the idea outright, I circled back and figured it wouldn't hurt to try, especially if it would help her feel at home in the water. Now, bathing together is special time. I'm so grateful I took the plunge—with her.

~Miriam, mom to Dalia

Frequency of Bathing

We're told to sponge bathe our newborns in order to allow the umbilical cord to heal. Weekly baths are the norm, using soap sparingly. As babies get older though, many parents switch to daily baths to help lull little ones into nighttime sleep. Most parents believe that daily baths are essential to infant hygiene.

But here's another way to look at it. Ever been told by your hairdresser that your hair is damaged from being washed too often? Just like adults, babies are often over-washed. Not only do most babies not need their hair washed more than once per week—unless they've been soiled in some creative way—but a weekly bath is usually enough, too. Most data on over-bathing focuses on preemies, who tend to be given daily baths in the hospital despite ill effects.[20] That said, you'll want to regularly clean those tricky crevices where the sun doesn't shine, and where bacteria can grow. That includes newborn neck folds and the skin where thigh meets groin. Keeping the genital area fresh and aired out is key to preventing rashes and infections, too. Don't forget those chubby little hands! They should be wiped down multiple times a day, especially if you have a crawler. Though we have faith in your house-cleaning abilities, dust and dirt often accumulate faster than we can vacuum!

As babies become more mobile and those chubby fingers start fixin' mud pies, some moms increase their frequency of bathing. You might find you love bonding in the bath, and look forward to the regular time together.

Body Care Products

Sad newsflash—traditional baby care products carry toxins. Lots of 'em. The U.S. government doesn't require cosmetics manufacturers to test for safety before they go to market, nor does the FDA regulate most ingredients, some of which have been linked to cancer and other health conditions.[21, 22] Europe has more stringent regulations, and often manufacturers of the same products will sell different versions to different countries.

We know that what we put on our skin, from scalp to toenails, enters the bloodstream. Especially when pregnant, even small amounts of toxic chemicals can mean big trouble for baby's developing system.[23] So, if your shampoo or body wash contains questionable ingredients, you may want to switch to safer products. We'll share the top three worst offenders here:

Fragrance. A catch-all phrase used to hide phthalates and other ingredients linked to adverse health issues.

Triclosan. An antibacterial and antifungal toxin and probable carcinogen used in many soaps and sanitizers.

Formaldehyde. A cancer-causing embalming tool.[24] You'll spot it by name or in related preservatives like diazolidinyl urea and imidazolidinyl urea.

A general rule of thumb for concerned moms? Check the label! Look for natural products whose ingredients you can recognize. In a baby's first year, all he needs is a gentle soap or body wash, ideally organic. No shampoo, conditioner or moisturizer necessary.

Babywearing

Touch is a vital way to ground babies. But most mamas would go nuts sitting inside holding a baby for months, no matter how cute he was. Enter babywearing. Gaining popularity among city slickers and country bumpkins alike, this age-old practice meets both mom's and baby's need to be in contact while going about their new life together.

While many Western mothers view strollers as their go-to accessory, carriers both predate and outperform their modern counterparts. Native cultures know that babywearing does wonders for both babies and mothers. We admit—strollers are functional. They get babies from place to place, soothe them through womb-like motion, and offer a place to rest while mama goes about her business. But carriers do all that *and* offer closeness to mama. Not only does the carrier free mom to use her hands and get to work (or play!), it promotes bonding and health. A study found that babies who were carried at least three hours per day cried 43% less in duration than babies who were carried a "normal" amount.[25]

Picking a carrier can be daunting. We'll give you some key safety tips, and blow the horn on a few major trends in the carrier market.

Benefits of Upright Carrying

By Elizabeth Antunovic, Founder of Boba, Inc.

With a baby upright on his mother's body, mom adjusts to all her baby's movements, and he to hers, moving like perfect dance partners. Constant feedback from his skin and the fluid in his inner ear help the baby understand space, and his place in it. A baby's muscles become stronger as they respond to the varied movement of mom's body and the force of gravity.

It's no surprise that babies carried upright scored higher on both motor and mental tests in the first year of life. The rich environment worked the babies' neural pathways.

Carrying a baby upright on your chest regulates his autonomic system. Studies have shown that a baby's heart rate stabilizes, his body temperature regulates, he transitions more easily from one sleep state to another, and actually sleeps longer. His breathing becomes steady, he has less chance of apnea, and oxygenation of his body increases. While on his mother's chest, his systems are kept at a regular tempo. When apart from his mother, a baby works twice as hard to maintain physiological harmony.

A mother can trust her intuition. By holding her baby close to her heart, she uses the most physiologically beneficial method of carrying her baby, providing the optimal environment for her baby's psychological and emotional growth.

The Scoop on Safety

As babywearing grows in popularity, Western moms are learning to the how-to's from pamphlets, YouTube, and trial and error. Without a line of mamas to pass down the art of babywearing from generation to generation, our cultural wisdom about safety has been lost. As a result, we've seen some tragic baby deaths and injuries in carriers.

While it's important to blow the whistle on unsafe babywearing practices, it's all too easy to throw out the baby carrier with the bathwater. Babywearing is safe, if done safely. We'll share tips on where to be especially careful.

Keeping Airways Clear

Your baby's windpipe is about the size of a straw. We'll state the obvious: it's critical that he can breathe easily at all times. Babies at the highest risk of suffocation are under four months old, or were born prematurely, with low birth-weight, or with other medical problems.

Here are some common-sense tips that apply to babies at any age. When a baby is reclined in a sling-type carrier on his back with his head near your chest,[1] keep his airway clear.

1. It's dangerous for his chin to touch his chest. The width of your finger should fit between his chin and his chest. If the baby's back is curved, like it would be if he were in the fetal position, there may be a problem.
2. Keep nose and mouth clear. Make sure the fabric of the sling and your body (especially breasts) don't block his breathing.
3. A baby should sit high in the carrier, facing you, so you can see his face at all times. A good rule of thumb is to keep him close enough to kiss his forehead.

Ring slings are popular carriers. Part of their appeal for moms with younger babies is that slings are simple to pull on and off, and easy to nurse in. But babies are safest in an upright position. If you nurse your baby—carefully and attentively—in the cradle hold, reposition him before moving on to your next task.

Overheard...

As a newborn, Kylie was in a carrier or held the majority of the time—not because I understood the benefits of babywearing, but because anytime I put her down she cried. My instinct told me it was the right thing to do. Once she became mobile, the carrier was still magical for calming her down when she was upset, and helping her fall asleep.

~Tricia, mom to Kylie and Mason

---

[1] Known as the cradle hold, typically used for nursing

Spinal Pressure

What we're about to share is news to many, but common knowledge to babywearing fanatics. When held upright in a carrier, a baby's butt must be lower than his knees for his hips to develop properly. In other words, babies should be carried in a squatting position. [26]

The most popular baby carrier on the American market is famous for its versatility—the baby can face forward or backwards. While options are usually a good thing, in this case, we'd caution you. Many carriers are "crotch danglers:" all the baby's weight sits on his crotch, putting harmful pressure on his spine. To illustrate—if you put yourself in his chubby little body, we'd bet you'd rather sit on a hammock than a thong.

On top of lacking proper physical support, babies who face outwards are more easily over-stimulated. Particularly during the first three months, babies will look away when they've had too much activity. In an outward-facing carrier, there's nowhere else to look, and mama might not notice her baby's distress. The baby doesn't know how to screen out all of the chaos, which can be overwhelming.

In a recent study, babies who faced outwards in strollers had elevated heart rates and were stressed out, factors that can lead to anxiety in adulthood. [27] When riding in inward-facing strollers, babies were two times more likely to interact with their caregivers, laugh, and fall asleep. Anecdotes from babywearing mamas and common sense tell us the same is true of carriers. Even so, some babies love facing outward. As long as you can position the baby's spine safely—butt below knees—and limit the amount of time he faces outward, feel free to respond to how he wants to be carried.

Overheard...

With my baby close to me in the carrier, she's more secure and content. I can sense and feel most of her needs and thus tend to her immediately; I can talk and sing to her when we're out walking; or pat and soothe her when she's about to fall asleep.

~Chialin, mom to Veronica and Antonia

Post-Adoption Carrier Bonding

By Maura Macfeat

When William first came to us he bonded right away to my husband, Michael. He loved going on adventures with him. He would say to me, "We are going—you stay here." I tried really hard not to take it personally, but I'm not going to lie—it hurt.

As Michael began working more, William and I started spending more time together. Living in the city requires a lot of walking. I tried a stroller but navigating busy streets was not easy. After one frustrating trip, I remembered the Mei Tai I had stashed in my closet. I pulled it out, tossed William on my back, and he loved it.

This was amazing because before this he didn't want to be held close. If I hugged him too long, he would get upset and pull away. Having him this close to me was so treasured. It felt like we were bonding and he didn't even know it. I finally found a way to be close to my new son. It was the missing piece to our parenting puzzle.

I wore William every day that he was four. I am so glad to have found babywearing when I did. I felt him pulling away and through babywearing I was able to pull him back in.

Pick That Baby Up!

Scientists and mamas around the world agree: babies are meant to be cuddled. Our instincts tell us to stroke his skin, carry him close, and soothe his tears. Mother nurture's benefits are exponential. The more you heed the call of your heart, the more you'll hear its soft beat. Soon you'll be listening in stereo to your instincts and your baby's needs—like you were born to do it.

Lest you think it's all about your baby though, rest assured. We get a kickback, too. Another sweet effect of nurturing your baby with the power of touch is that you activate your own feel-good hormones and endorphins. There's nothing closer to a win-win.

Milk
feed with love

Breastfeeding is one of the most amazing powers a mother has, second maybe to incubating and birthing new life. Breast milk is a mama's maverick: it provides perfectly for a baby's daily nourishment needs, and changes its contents to amp up antibodies when illness is detected. Mother's milk is a comforting, delicious food that adapts its volume to suit a baby's appetite and meets his nutritional needs perfectly.

We want to be clear: it is not our intention to apply any more pressure on mothers already struggling with judgment, no matter what choice they make. But at the same time, we can't deny that research, experience, and history all point to breastfeeding as the healthiest way to feed babies. We recognize that some women are not in a position to exclusively or even partially breastfeed. But solidarity around breastfeeding education and nursing rights is important. Read on and perhaps you'll be armed with information to support a mom who needs you.

You won't find a how-to guide for breastfeeding in the following pages. If you don't already know about latches and positions, you're much better served by professionals, mothers, sisters, friends or support groups. Breastfeeding is a learned skill, and takes on-the-job training. Instead, we'll navigate the muddled history of society's relationship with nursing moms. We'll touch on the early days with your nursling, addressing hot topics like pacifying, feeding frequency, and milk supply. We'll meet the formula industry head on, and share information to help you make the best decision for you and your baby.

The Breastfeeding Boon

Choosing between breast milk and formula isn't like choosing between Coke and Pepsi. Stacks of studies confirm why babies (and mamas!) need to nurse, and why formula is a poor substitute. But formula can sustain a baby's life, and sometimes it's needed. We get that.

Most Western moms try breastfeeding immediately after birth, but it's helpful to know just how awesome your milk is, whether to confirm your intuition, make a decision, or give you ammo when someone pressures you to offer a bottle of milk substitute.

Nature's perfect medicine. Breast milk protects babies against disease, illness, and allergies.[1] Diarrhea and vomiting are much higher in formula-fed babies, which translates to more frequent doctor's visits. More importantly, healthy babies are happy babies. And happy babies make for happy mamas.

Brains and brawn. The DHA (omega-3 fatty acids) in breast milk supports your little one's developing IQ. Babies given breast milk in their first weeks had a significantly higher IQ by age seven,[2] and more advanced social and motor skills.[3]

Nice smile. Sucking at the breast uses different muscles than sucking at a bottle. Formula-fed infants don't get the jaw, teeth, facial muscles, and speech development benefits that they would get from nursing.[4] This can translate to lower dentist bills for breastfed babies.[5]

Cancer stopper. Women who don't breastfeed have higher rates of breast and ovarian cancer. One study found that if all women with children lactated for more than two years, breast cancer may be reduced by a whopping 25 percent![6]

Overheard...

One unexpected benefit of nursing is that I got to know my body much better. Before breastfeeding, I rarely did self-exams, and had no idea what I was doing. Now, I'm confident that if there were a perceptible issue (my family has a history of breast cancer) I'd know right away.

~Andrea, mom to Jane

Time saver. If your baby's hungry at midnight, in the mall, or during a phone conversation, you're fully equipped to feed him in less than two seconds, give or take cover-up time for modest moms. That's priceless.

Natural birth control. Around the world, breastfeeding moms have a secret: let baby fulfill all sucking needs at the breast day and night, skip pacifiers, and you have a recipe for natural child spacing. Around the world, most moms who use this method, called ecological breastfeeding, have a 1% chance of conceiving during the first six months.[7] But a higher percentage of U.S. moms get pregnant in the first six months. It's likely due to a mix of factors like diet, lifestyle and genetics. So, until more research is done, it's best to use backup.

No carbon offsets necessary. Even organic formula majorly taxes the planet. Packaging, BPA-lined cans, methane gas from cows, land and feed for cows, gas to harvest cow feed and bring milk to factories, refrigerated storage: their effect is part of our final cost.

Delayed, period. Most breastfeeding mamas don't get their periods for a while, also known as lactational amenorrhea. For moms who breastfeed around the clock, their period returns in an average of 15 months.[8] Moms who want to get pregnant right away may not appreciate it, but the rest of us dig the time off.

Love. We saved the best for last. Of course you can bond with your bottle-fed baby. But biologically, you get an advantage putting your baby to the breast. Mothering hormones oxytocin and prolactin are released to help us relax, feel good, and bond with our babies. Take that, Zoloft!

Overheard...

I could not believe the blissed-out feelings I got from nursing! What was surprisingly amazing was the depth of connection to my baby and the feeling of awe that I could be there for him in such an immediate and profound way. Just the BEST!

~Rachel, mom to Sean

Just One Sip

By Nancy Holtzman, RN, IBCLC, VP at Isis Parenting

Many parents don't know that introducing formula, especially when a baby is younger than three or four months, actually interferes with the baby's immune system by changing properties of the digestive tract.

Infants' digestive tracts are the front line of their immune system. Introducing formula—yes, even one bottle—has implications. This isn't a judgment. It's simply clinical fact. Formula alters the delicate pH balance of the breastfed baby's GI tract and changes beneficial gut flora that helps newborns fight infection.[9] Formula also introduces (and potentially sensitizes) the infant to foreign proteins, especially cows' milk protein and soy protein, two of the most common allergens for infants.[10] Early introduction of these substances may set up a susceptible baby for asthma, eczema, allergies or even diabetes down the road. These illnesses could possibly have been avoided if the protein were introduced later when the intestinal lining was more mature. This isn't some opinion, it's data found in hundreds of credible studies frequently published in the most reputable medical journals.

Sometimes formula is necessary. Nobody is suggesting that we withhold food from a hungry baby! But parents and caregivers need to understand the significance of casual early supplementation.

As medical professionals and parents become more aware, and banked human milk more available, some NICUs and hospitals keep frozen human milk available for when supplementation is needed.

The benefits of breastfeeding are dose-dependent. A day of colostrum is better than none, a week of breast milk is better than a day, and a month is better than a week. But parents should know that the benefits of nursing are strongest when breast milk is exclusive.

Wouldn't you be furious if a nurse casually offered to give your baby a bottle of formula in the nursery to let you sleep, when that single bottle of formula could lead to a childhood of asthma? What if a pediatrician suggested "topping off a feed" with an ounce or two of formula, never mentioning that it might introduce a protein linked to the development of diabetes? Where is informed consent?

Skinny minnies. Let's get real. Extra baby weight can be a drag. Breastfeeding burns about 400–500 calories a day.[11] You can almost justify skipping the gym.

Reframing Normal

We never hear the hazards of not breastfeeding. The benefits of nursing are usually framed as bonuses. Your child will have "fewer ear infections" or "better digestive health." But breastfeeding is the norm that Mother Nature has delivered to thriving generations of humans and other mammals throughout history. Just as we assess the harms of new practices like injecting cows with antibiotics, substituting formula for breast milk presents well-established health risks for both mother and child, even in the Western world. No one wants to hear that their formula-fed baby will have "more ear infections," or "sub-par digestive health," but that's precisely what is happening. Only when we present the true colors of nursing and formula-feeding, can we say we have given women a real choice.

Overheard...

While pregnant, I actually told friends that I hoped I wouldn't be able to breastfeed, because I wanted to share responsibility for late night feedings. No one ever told me that Dalia's gut would be permanently altered by formula. But on the fourth day of her life, I found myself crying hysterically because I didn't have enough milk.

My Lactation Consultant confirmed that I wasn't providing enough nourishment. We invested in organic formula, and I worked to increase my supply. After two months, I was feeding Dalia all on my own. People were incredulous that I weaned her off of formula—most do the opposite. The top trick for increasing supply was the one my LC didn't share: co-sleeping. The nighttime hours when Dalia nursed as often as she wanted got us back on track.

~Miriam, mom to Dalia

PACIFIER BEWARE

Introducing a pacifier before feeding is well established can harm your milk supply and your nursing relationship![12] Conversely, letting your baby nurse and pacify at will is the best way to build your milk supply. And it's way more pleasant than the pump!

The Early Days

While some people sail through the early days and weeks of breastfeeding, most mothers hit a bump or two in the road. Unfortunately, there's no "Easy" button for breastfeeding. We'll give you the scoop on some common issues and a few tips to help you overcome them naturally.

On Cue

Some moms are shocked after learning their newborn needs to nurse around 12 times a day for optimal growth and development. It may seem like a lot, but babies double their size in the first six months, and they need a lot of nourishment to get there. While popular parenting books from the 80s and 90s (and even today!) advise us to schedule feedings, studies are clear this isn't best for babies or moms.[13] One study even found that babies fed on schedule scored four points lower on IQ tests in early childhood![14]

Scheduled feedings can confuse and frustrate babies. Science agrees with what every baby knows: babies can self-regulate their food intake.[15] When well-intentioned moms may impose limits or structure around feedings, externally-imposed schedules can override the baby's self-regulation.

Instead of recording feed times and setting your alarm, there's a much easier way: watch your baby. It's important to follow his lead. Delaying a nursing session leaves mom at a higher risk of engorgement, breast infection, and low supply. Babies fare even worse. Their tiny tummies digest breast milk within 1–2 hours, so they're hungry often. Newborns also may cluster feed, nursing several times in a row, then sleep for several hours. Mother nature knew what she was doing when she taught babies to nurse at night: growth hormones peak while asleep.

Some experts distinguish between nutritive and non-nutritive nursing, but that language is misleading. Nutritive means nourishing, and when your baby's full but wants closeness— that nourishes him, too. You're giving the gifts of security and love. Whether he ate an hour ago, or five minutes ago, feel free to offer the breast. Remember, you can't overfeed a nursing baby!

Reading Feeding Cues

Ideally, you want to be prepared to nurse your babe when he's just starting to ask. If he's escalated to crying, that's a late hunger cue, and he's in need of mama milk!

Starting to feel a rumble...
• Lip-licking and smacking
• Mouth opening and closing
• Sucking on fingers, toes, or other object

Ready to go, Mama.
• For newborns, simply waking up is a cue
• Rooting around for a nipple
• Squirming
• Tapping or hitting your arm or chest (in that sweet baby way, of course)
• Rapid breathing

Feed me, now!
• Crying
• Frantic movements

Okay, so now you know when to feed, but what about when to finish? This is easier to figure out. Baby-led feedings are often baby-finished too. If your little one pops off spontaneously, you can try burping and offering the other side, but don't push if he doesn't want to latch. Babies often fall asleep at the breast, so if your nipple falls out, or the suck pattern is very slow, it's likely time to take a snooze. Or you can gently stick your little finger in the corner of your babe's mouth to break the suction.

Supply and Demand

The most common reason moms cite for weaning is low supply. If we perceive low supply, it's usually a matter of confidence or technique, rather than a legitimate medical issue.

Before you write off your girls as slackers, check these telltale signs that nursing is going well:
- Your newborn has frequent eliminations
- The baby appears full and satisfied after feeding
- That little eating machine is gaining weight.

Just because you're not leaking milk doesn't mean you aren't making enough milk. But if you checked no for any of the variables above, we recommend you seek help. If there is a supply issue, it's usually easily remedied through technique. An expert can check the baby's latch, suck pattern, or position, and give a helpful fix.

If your little one's latch is perfect but you're still skeptical about your milk production, make note of how often you're nursing. Supply is a direct function of demand. If demand is high (i.e. lots of boob time), your body will work to keep up. Going three or more hours between feeds can signal your milk-makers to slow down. Here are a few tips to keep your milk flowing:

Offer often! Our breasts contain bundles of nerves (just like us during those first few days...) that signal the milk-making and transporting parts to get working! If your babe has free access to milk and a vigorous suck, he'll reach deeper nerves, which trigger milk-releasing hormones. Conversely a sleepy, barely-nursing baby or one with an improper latch, may not be able to stimulate the deeper nerves, leading to less milk production and release.

Get close. Wear your baby skin-to-skin if possible. Co-bathing also encourages nursing. If you have the flexibility, try a "nursing moon"— bunk up together for a day or two and spend your time nursing, sleeping, and...nursing.

Switch power. Rapidly switching sides while nursing can help bring in your milk faster.

Co-sleep. Working moms in particular can keep their supply strong by giving their babe access to the breast throughout the night. A bonus? The prolactin released while nursing will help you doze off quickly.

Herbal supplements. Many lactation consultants and nursing mamas across the globe recommend fenugreek, raspberry leaf, goat's rue and blessed thistle. Some foods, like asparagus, almonds, oatmeal and brewer's yeast, are considered galactagogues—milk boosters.

Drink up. Make sure you're hydrated. Coffee, caffeinated tea, and juices don't count. A healthy amount of water is the best nursing fuel.

Can *touch this!* Hand expressing, breast compressions and pumping after nursing can also increase supply.

Decreasing

Given the buzz about low supply, it can be hard to believe some moms experience an oversupply. Too much milk is often coupled with strong let down: a fast and furious flow at the start of a nursing session. While it may not sound too bad in theory, when mamas have too much milk, babies can fuss at the breast, pop on and off, and be gassy and irritable. Seeing a professional Lactation Consultant is recommended, but these suggestions may start you off in the right direction.

Heads up. Nurse in an upright position, like in a carrier, which can help prevent gagging and sputtering.

Take a breather. Gently de-latch your baby when your milk lets down, and catch in a cloth until the flow slows.

Block it out. Instead of switching sides during the same nursing period, feed your baby as much as he wants from the same side during a two-to-three hour block. At the next feeding, offer the other side.[16]

The Nursing Cove

There are only two things you need to nurse your baby, and you'll be hard pressed to lose them. But in those early days, when newborns nurse 10, 12, 14 times a day—and sometimes for 40-60 minutes at a time—having a cozy space stocked with nursing mama goodies is a must-have!

Comfy spot. You'll be spending a lot of time here, so make sure you have a good spot to relax and nurse. No need to buy a new chair—a corner of your couch, an old rocking chair, or a repurposed armchair will do.

Water. New nursing moms get thirsty. Very thirsty. So keep several bottles of water near you at all times. There's nothing more frustrating than sitting down for a nursing session and feeling a wave of thirst come over you, with no water in sight.

Food. To keep you properly fueled, stash some high protein snacks, such as grass-fed dried beef sticks, whole fruit, nuts and dried fruit, or your favorite healthy energy bar (we heart Larabars) in a small basket near your spot.

Pillows. Breastfeeding pillows can be handy, but they also comply with flammability requirements that have toxic chemicals on them. So if you do use a breastfeeding pillow, toss a blanket over it first. You can also round up a few bed pillows (buckwheat work best), or thick, rolled up, organic blankets, and place them strategically under your arms. You'll get the hang of nursing without props, but they may be indispensable at first.

Nursing stool. The slanted design reduces strain on your back, legs, and hips. Rolled towels or phone books work in a pinch.

Cloths. Some mamas have a forceful let-down, and when the baby pulls off, milk sprays everywhere. Having a few cloths handy can minimize the mess of extra milk or spit up.

Reading material. You'll be sitting still for many, many hours. Why not catch up on some reading? For variety, stock up on your favorite magazines, newspapers, classics, and *The Other Baby Book!* Audiobooks allow you to relax and feed your mind while feeding your baby.

Nursing Strikes

What Gives? Sometimes babies take a break from nursing, and their mothers are left with little explanation. It is very rare that a baby under a year is "self-weaning." Any sudden refusal of the breast is not a self-weaning. Several issues may be the culprit. Do any of these reasons sound familiar?

- The baby has a cold, ear infection, or is teething, making nursing uncomfortable.
- A disruption in his schedule, like mom returning to work, a move, holidays or overnight guests.
- Baby bit mom, and because of her reaction is scared to nurse.
- Milk tastes different due to medication or pregnancy.
- Mom used a new soap or perfume and smells different.

Solutions. How do you make it through a nursing strike? Our seasoned panel of moms offers the following tips:

- Try nursing when your baby is drowsy, either falling asleep or just waking up.
- Take your baby into the bath. The warm skin-to-skin contact encourages nursing.
- Offer to nurse, but don't force. Make yourself available if your little one is interested.
- Nurse with your baby in an upright position, such as in a carrier, and if possible, go shirtless.
- Pump or hand express frequently, and feed in a bottle or cup.
- Go for a walk or meet up with friends. Leave the house so you are not consumed with how much milk your baby is drinking.
- Above all, don't stress. It'll likely pass in under a week. Call a doctor if your baby shows signs of dehydration, like fewer pees.

The Human Pacifier

We've all heard it: "Don't let your baby use you as a pacifier." Unlike the chicken and the egg, however, we know that mothers came first, pacis second. Pacifiers were made to stand in for mom. Our favorite response? "I'm not pacifying, I'm mothering."

Wonder why babies always root for something to suck? It's a survival reflex, ensuring babies are born with the ability to feed. It also helps babies secure the in-arms nurturing so crucial to survival. Their need to suck isn't always linked to hunger. Since most moms don't hold their babies 24/7, the pacifier became a substitute. But if you're a breastfeeding, babywearing, co-sleeping mama, you're well-positioned to fulfill his needs without a rubber binky.

Ever heard that tribal African babies never cry? Here's their secret. At any sign of distress, the breast is offered. Yes, their moms live differently than we do, but many Westerners find ways to mimic traditional habits. For those of us who have maternity leave, the first months can be used to nurture a baby with physical closeness.

The Social Side

At a time when breasts are considered eye candy or sexual props, and referred to casually in language that ranges from irreverent to obscene, when they're enlarged, reduced, propped up and put on display, it's easy to forget that breasts were designed to nourish life. Depending upon where you live, there are laws against showing our bare chest in public, but there are also laws protecting moms' right to feed our babies in public. Confusing? Yes.

Throughout the U.S., breastfeeding is legal and 45 states explicitly protect a mother's right to breastfeed with special legal provisions. Australia and the UK recently passed laws protecting women's rights to breastfeed. But those societies which are most technologically advanced also tend to have higher saturation of formula marketing.

Many laws don't require nursing mamas to cover up. But some women feel more comfortable this way. Most Western moms have been raised in a bottle-feeding culture that shaped our thinking about exposed breasts. But men in other countries—and women for that matter—don't bat an eye when a mom nurses uncovered.

Some moms are sensitive to arousing men. You may have heard that during the Victorian era, the sight of a woman's bare ankle was scandalous. And of course because the ankle was forbidden, it was subject to intense curiosity. Perhaps the more we breastfeed our babies in public, the less taboo the female breast will be.

Overheard...

It's up to the mom if she wants to cover up. Breasts were made to nourish and sustain life! How is it OK to stare at a teenage girl with a low cut shirt, but a mom nursing in public is unacceptable? Breasts being used to feed babies is the image we should portray to our sons so they will view women's bodies as much more than sexual objects.

~Lani, mom to Bentley

I was at lunch with my mom when my three-month-old decided he was ready to eat. My mother was incredulous and unhappy that I was going to nurse at the table. I was about to explain that it was very common and no one would mind when two ladies gave me a big thumbs up. Then the woman next to us said, "Oh, that's so lovely!" A moment later, a man told me how nice it was to see a mother bonding with her baby. My mom was still embarrassed, but she never said another word to me about not nursing in public!

~Courtney, mom to Mac and Liam

Pumping Love: Working and Breastfeeding

"Our society expects mothers to do six impossible things before breakfast, and then encourages women to feel guilty when they can't. ...We need to remove the barriers to breastfeeding–lack of support, lack of maternity leave, lack of workplace flexibility, poor advice from uninformed doctors, and lack of access to professional breastfeeding help."   *~Jessica Kosa*

Mamas who work and nurse put lots of time and energy into making sure their babies' nutritional needs are covered around the clock. Unless you have daycare on-site, pumping milk is inevitably part of the package. We've rounded up the best tips from our working moms panel to help you thrive.

Establish a routine. When you do re-enter the workforce, block out specific times to pump each day. Make sure you have the privacy and space you need, complete with an electrical outlet, lots of water and a comfy chair.

Enjoy your little one. If you have a maternity leave, the last thing you'll want to do is pump. Many babes don't even want freezer milk, and some won't take a bottle. Pump a day or two ahead of time at work and enjoy your baby while on your leave.

Speak up. Advocate for your needs. Let your coworkers know what will and won't work for your schedule. It's rare that one's officemates will get exactly what goes into pumping.

Overheard...

It's really important to stand up for what you need. If you are invited to an all-day meeting, say that you are taking breaks and just do it You don't have to explain why—if people know you're a new mom and you just say pointedly, "No, we can't skip lunch—I need that 30 minute lunch break," people get the hint.

~Shannon, mom to Kai

Nurse at home. Moms who can work from home one or more days per workweek are able to boost their supply (and enjoyment) by nursing their baby from the source. Mornings, evenings and weekends are also optimal times to reconnect.

Overheard...

There were times my supply waned because I was sick, or we both got thrush. When that happened, I would have nursing weekends where we spent all day cuddling and nursing.

~Hannah, mom to Juliet

Invest in success. Though some do best hand-expressing into a bottle, most working moms swear by their high quality, double duty breast pump. Other accessories like a hands-free pumping bra, specially-sized flanges, spare pump parts to cut down on washing, as well as extra bottles and milk storage bags, will make managing the details of working and pumping a little easier.

Remember to eat. Life gets hectic, but don't skip meals! Most moms do best on three square meals, along with several high-quality snacks each day. And keep your water bottle handy.

Breastfeeding and working outside of the home is hard, and brave mamas who rise to the occasion are pretty heroic, in our book.

Milk Alternatives

There's an overwhelming sentiment in the mothersphere that all women can feed their babies from the breast. If at first they don't succeed, try, try again…then buy some herbs and go topless as much as possible, so baby has easy access to milk. But what if that's not true? Sometimes, breastfeeding your baby just isn't going to happen, whether it be for medical reasons on your end, your baby's, or extraordinary circumstances. In those cases, many turn to formula, but believe it or not we have options that don't come in cans.

The World Health Organization (WHO) ranks the healthiest baby-feeding practices. Breast milk direct from the baby's mother is best. Second is expressed or pumped milk from the baby's mom. If that's not possible, the WHO recommends milk from another healthy mama in the form of a wet nurse or a milk bank. Closing out the list in the fourth and final spot are artificial milk substitutes.

Milk Sharing

Way-back-when, it was common to see mamas with a healthy milk supply breastfeed babies not their own. But in our sue-happy society, it can be a stretch to imagine offering even a bottle of your breast milk to another baby.

Megan, A Novel Mama

Tales from the Trenches

When Anabella was three weeks old, I wrote down some book titles I wanted to use if ever I got the chance to put on a shirt and pick up a pen. Motherhood: A Soggy Journey, Dripping My Way Through The Hours, *and* The Clothes in My Closet...And Other Useless Items. *Breastfeeding consumed us. It was our morning, our afternoon, our evening, and all night.*

Before my girl came, I read voraciously about pain-free deliveries, cloth diapering options, and organic mattresses. Breastfeeding, I thought, would just come naturally. Women have nipples, babies have mouths—how hard could it be? At four months pregnant, I began attending La Leche League meetings to meet other breastfeeding mamas and get a few last-minute tips. I thought I had it in the bag, so when a leader suggested I read The Womanly Art of Breastfeeding, *I irreverently responded, "Someone wrote a whole book about breastfeeding?" My ignorance was glaring.*

A few months later, propped up on a lumpy hospital bed, getting my lady parts stitched up, words from websites and baby books swirled around my head. Anxiety kicked in full-gear. Shouldn't I bring the baby to my breast right now? Isn't she starving? Didn't she need to drink colostrum or else she'd end up with asthma, jaundice, and probably be allergic to nuts, wheat and dairy?? Nurses were swatting my hands and telling me the baby wasn't hungry and didn't want to eat just yet.

Everything was a blur. I was armed with ignorance and hope, and neither prepared me for latching on my baby.

I wished I had read The Womanly Art of Breastfeeding.

The first days and weeks of nursing were challenging. Not everyone has a hard time of it, but I couldn't wear a shirt or take a shower, or hug my husband for weeks. My breasts felt like cement bowling balls stitched onto my body. I lived with cabbage leaves in my bra to relieve the pain of engorgement, and used hot, salty water to soothe my burning nipples.

I got mastitis, a breast infection complete with fever and "I-just-got-hit-by-a-truck" symptoms. Three times.

But homeopathy, copious amounts of raw garlic, a food known for its anti-viral properties, and frequent nursing overcame the infections.

Despite the bumps in the road, there was never a time when I thought, I can't do this anymore. But there were many moments when I figured I'd just quietly suffer through our nursing relationship until she weaned.

Of course, within a month, my nipples were healed. Now, the moments we share while Anabella nurses are among the most precious of my life. Nothing could have prepared me for the love I feel when she gazes into my eyes and pats my breasts, content to be. Not even The Womanly Art of Breastfeeding.

Wet Nurses

Milk sharing is an old practice, no doubt. The idea of a wet nurse goes back several thousand years. These women were generally of a lower social class, or relatives of the nursling. Today, milk sharing still exists. Some women who choose this option prefer their baby nursing from someone they know, and opt for a friend or relative. Others would rather bond with their baby via a bottle of milk from a donor. Still others with no milk go to great lengths to feed their babies with a lactation aid, like a tube, so that their little ones can gain the benefits of suckling at mom's breast, and drinking breast milk.

Milk Banks

This healthy option was made possible after the breast pump arrived in 1863. Women could produce and remove milk from their breasts in large quantities. The first milk bank was established in 1909 in Vienna, giving mothers a place to buy and sell breast milk. Women seeking a few extra coins sold their milk to these banks across Europe and North America. But by the end of World War II, infant formula was promoted as better for babies. So milk banks fell out of favor. After the AIDS crisis, milk banks were almost obsolete. (HIV can pass from mom to baby through breast milk.)

Today, human milk is growing in popularity as research confirms its superiority over milk substitutes. From 2000–2008, distribution in North America alone rose 185%! Like blood banks, milk banks extensively screen donors, then carefully process, freeze, and distribute the milk. It doesn't come cheap: at $2-4 an ounce, a weekly feeding bill could run $300–400. (Keep in mind, though, some moms spend that much on high end formula.) Most milk bank milk is distributed to hospitals for premature babies. If it's a medical necessity, private medical insurance may foot the bill.

If you don't have lots of extra cash, check out MilkShare. This organization serves as a connection point for moms who want to explore private milk donation. Moms in need only pay for bags and shipping—the milk is free, but also lacks the secure screening. Viruses like HIV and hepatitis are transmitted through breast milk, so be sure to vet any potential donors independently.

Overheard...

I started pumping right away, just in case. After a few weeks, I realized I was pumping 30 ounces a day and my freezer stash wasn't getting any smaller! I looked into donating, and met a woman through MilkShare. She'd had prior breast surgery and barely produced any milk. She refused to give her baby commercial formula, so she used donated milk and made formula using raw goats' milk as well. I'd nurse her baby boy when she came to pick up the milk, so she'd have that extra feeding of frozen milk. Every little bit helps.

~Lani, mom to Bentley

The Formula Fallacy

Of course, there are medical exceptions and extraordinary circumstances (and we know wonderful, loving moms in each of those categories!) that factor into a mother's choice not to breastfeed. But some moms have been sold a story that simply isn't true. Guess who's been selling that false story, quite profitably?

The formula industry.

Formula companies have run one of the most successful anti-public-health campaigns in the history of the world. The formula industry is currently worth billions of dollars. And the ill effects of this chemical food product cost us billions as well. One study estimates that the U.S. alone could save $13 billion a year in health care dollars if moms chose breast over bottle in the early months.[17] The formula empire's marketing strategies undermine women's ability to provide for their babies by implying that infants need more than just breast milk for optimal health and nourishment. Another dangerous—and false—message is that the chemical makeup of artificial formula is very close to breast milk.

We know breast milk is baby's tried and true best food, but it's especially important for those who are starting off with less access to quality (and often times expensive) food. Unfortunately, the babies who most need mama's milk aren't getting it. The U.S. government purchases more than half of all infant formula consumed in the U.S. for its poorest families! If mothers meet the income criteria, they're given supplies of free formula. Moms in other countries are not so "lucky." Some governments, like Australia, no longer subsidize formula.

Official reports are clear: formula companies make a substantial profit off of low-income women. One study conducted in the U.S. put taxpayer spending on subsidized formula and government health aid at $590 million per year![18] We think that's money better spent on direct human services rather than padding the pocket of a rich industry.[19]

It's not just mamas in need who suffer from this lopsided marketing. The World Health Organization's 1981 International Code of Marketing of Breast-Milk Substitutes is often violated by formula companies, with no enforcement by many governments. The code prohibits manufacturers from targeting all moms through free formula samples, mailings, or any other type of advertising or promotion. But many new mothers receive "gifts" of discharge packs from the hospital with formula samples for the baby.

What the formula companies are not packing with their powdered milk freebies is the real story. Researchers funded by formula companies conceded, "[It is] increasingly apparent that infant formula can never duplicate human milk. Human milk contains living cells, hormones, active enzymes, immunoglobulins and compounds with unique structures that cannot be replicated in infant formula."[20]

It's hard to imagine that, given the right support, so many moms would choose not to breastfeed. It's so hard to imagine actually, that we'll venture to say they really weren't given a choice. But inadequate information about the hazards of *not* nursing does not a choice make.

Formula has been recalled many times, with some incidents of accidental contamination, and some profit-motivated. In 2008 a global formula recall was due to widespread contamination by melamine, a substance that, according to the Material Safety Data Sheet, is "harmful if swallowed, inhaled or absorbed through the skin. Chronic exposure may cause cancer or reproductive damage."[21]

Today, nursing is on the rise, with roughly three-quarters of moms nursing their babies immediately after birth. But we're still advocating for increased support for mamas, as well as a rise in public awareness about the ways that formula can harm newborns' developing systems.

There will be some of you who have done research and soul-searching, and decided not to breastfeed, or circumstances demand you supplement with formula. Will you be forever shunned by your nursing friends (who, statistically speaking, will only be one out of five after a year anyway)? Shame, guilt, and condemnation are too often used on new moms. This, naturally, pushes moms who may have been on the fence, way over to the other side. Just writing this chapter was a struggle for us: how do we share the awesomeness of nursing without making non-nursing moms want to throw our book out window?

If formula's the route you're taking, you deserve quality information about your options, too. Breastfeeding education shouldn't be like abstinence education. Even though we hope one day every single mother will feed her baby breast milk for a year, the path there isn't to stick our head in the sand until we arrive. Let's rise to the challenge, and in the meantime, provide mothers with information to help them make the best decision for their formula-fed baby.

Support for Formula-Feeding Moms

If you're feeding your baby formula, we bet you want it to be the healthiest on the market. We've got a few pointers if you're debating what to buy. Ultimately, the greatest factor in determining the optimal formula is your baby's response. While you're looking at the shelves, dizzy with choices, let these guidelines get you started.

Read ingredients. The more items you can pronounce and recognize, the closer to their original state they're likely to be. Overall, organic brands score better on this test. Plus, pesticides and new babies just don't mix.

Pick your protein ratio wisely. Breast milk is 80% whey to 20% casein, so try to stick close to this ratio for ideal digestion. If casein levels are high, babies tend to have gassiness and constipation.

Jury's out on DHA. Many formula companies have added omega oils DHA and ARA, which are extracted using hexane, a neurotoxin. It's not yet clear whether these synthetics help more than harm.[22]

Stay away from soy. Some pediatricians prescribe soy for babies with colic or allergies, but the AAP doesn't recommend it unless your baby is intolerant to the protein in milk, comes from a vegan family, or has galactosemia.[23] Babies with cow's milk allergies have high risks of soy allergies, and will better tolerate hydrolyzed protein formula. Small babies and preemies are cautioned not to drink soy formula because it interferes with bone growth.[24]

Benefits of Continued Nursing

Our focus is a baby's first 12 months, but we couldn't leave the first year of nursing without a sneak peek into the future. As we move beyond babyhood, some of us have clear ideas about what comes next and some don't. For those of us who live in countries where doctors only recommend breastfeeding for the first six months, and few moms continue after year one, it's helpful to hear the facts about nursing past the first birthday. So, when the lady at the grocery store tells you there's no benefit to "extended" nursing, let her chew on this...

Breast milk's nutrients don't dry up when a baby turns one. Babies thrive on mama milk's protein, fat, and vitamins well into their second year. In fact, world breastfeeding expert and biocultural anthropologist Kathy Dettwyler says, "At this point, all of the research that has been conducted on the health and cognitive consequences of different lengths of breastfeeding shows steadily increasing benefits the longer a child is breastfed...and no negative consequences."[25]

In the second year of life, two cups of breast milk fulfills the following dietary needs of an average toddler:[xviii]

- 94% of Vitamin B12
- 76% of Folate
- 75% of Vitamin A

- 60% of Vitamin C
- 43% of Protein
- 36% of Calcium
- 29% of Energy

Worried about iron? A study found that "Infants who were exclusively breastfed for a prolonged period had a good iron status at 12 and 24 months." The shorter the length of breastfeeding, the more likely babies were to be anemic.[26]

In a study of babies who nursed beyond a year, the shorter a child was nursed, the more behavior issues he had. Who wants to spend afternoons in the principal's office?[27]

The benefits of breastfeeding beyond a year aren't limited to babies. The longer a mama nurses, the lower her risk of cancer (breast,[28] uterine[29] and endometrial[30]), osteoporosis[31] and arthritis![32]

Instinct in Love

In an age where technology is used to save and enhance lives, we've also seen women stripped of power in arenas solely theirs: pregnancy, birth and breastfeeding. Instead of engaging in that sacred trio of life-giving acts, we may be spectators in a three-ring circus. Often corporations run the show, with a host of supporters. Precious few mamas are given the respect of knowing what's best for their baby.

But change is in the air. As more mamas rediscover the hidden gems of motherhood, babies are thriving and mother-baby relationships, deepening. Breastfeeding is not the only way to bond with your baby, but if you're able and can garner the support to make it happen, you'll enjoy one of the most natural pleasures known to women. Little else compares to that itty bird-like mouth popping around, looking for milk…or tiny hands kneading their source of nourishment…or watching the waves of contentment flow through your baby as he drinks in nature's finest.

Sleep
rest in security

Most Western babies sleep in cribs, but many parents don't realize that mom's bed can actually be safer and healthier. The thought of sharing a sleep surface may give you the willies, though. You've likely heard awful stories about suffocation, SIDS, and bachelors who sleep in their parents' bed. But remember, we're *The Other Baby Book*. We're here to present you with an alternative view. We'll catch you up on the latest research and oldest traditions around infant sleep, both of which agree: the crib may not be progressive after all. So let's explore one of the most time-honored baby care practices: co-sleeping.

In addition to where babies sleep, how long they sleep can be an obsession for many new moms. Sleeping through the night is the holy grail for most new parents. We've been programmed to think that if our baby sleeps soundly for ten hours in his own crib, we've achieved sleep success. But it's time to think again.

What if...

...our modern vision of newborn sleep has no basis in babies' biological needs, nor in how sleep and feeding develop?

...sleeping through the night is not at all what a baby needs (or even usually does) in the first four to eight months?

...not only does getting enough sleep makes a baby healthier and smarter, but also waking next to mom to feed?[1]

…a baby most needs two things: lots of nighttime breast milk (which is richer in fat, certain hormones and enzymes than daytime milk) and delivery through a mom sleeping close by, which has social, emotional and cognitive benefits?

Would it rock your cradle if we told you those "what if's" are true? We'll share more details in the coming pages. You'll get a healthy dose of sleep history to start. Then, we'll bulldoze a few myths, alleviate some fears, and share some benefits of bunking with your baby. You'll see a quick troubleshooting guide for some of the most common sleep concerns. Finally, if you'd like to give the family bed a try, you'll find a safe sleeping guide for your precious cargo.

A Peek into the Past

Get this. Aside from Western, industrialized countries, few babies sleep away from their moms. In a survey of a hundred societies, the only babies who slept in their own space were from the U.S.! Meredith Small, anthropologist and author of *Our Babies, Ourselves* says (perhaps more tactfully than this) the U.S. sticks out like a sore thumb when it comes to sleep. Westerners are the only ones who put babies in their own beds, in separate rooms.

According to *Sleeping with Your Baby: A Parent's Guide to Co-Sleeping* by Dr. James McKenna, a leading sleep researcher and Director of the University of Notre Dame Mother-Baby Behavioral Sleep Lab:

> *In Latin America, the Philippines, and Vietnam, some parents sleep with their baby in a hammock next to the bed. Others place their baby in a wicker basket in the bed, between the two parents. In Japan, many parents sleep next to their baby on bamboo or straw mats, or on futons. Some parents simply room-share by putting the baby in a crib or bassinet that is kept within arm's reach of the bed. Most cultures that routinely practice co-sleeping in any form, have very rare instances of SIDS. SIDS occurrences are among the lowest in the world in Hong Kong, where co-sleeping is extremely common.*

While it's true that many Western parents do prepare and use separate sleeping spaces for their babies, there is a growing segment of the population that brings their little one into bed. Quite likely one-half of all new parents share sleep for some or part of the night in the U.S. alone. A big reason that this shift has taken place is because of the connection between breastfeeding and sleep. Not only is it easier to not let your toes touch the ground when you hear that hungry squirm, nature also intended that you not have to.

In the recent past, cultural preferences determined who did and didn't share a sleep space. But as breastfeeding and co-sleeping move up in the charts, moms of all backgrounds are discovering that keeping their baby close makes night nursing easier and does wonders for regulating milk supply,[2] all while offering maximum sleep with minimal disruption.

Co-Sleeping Throughout Time

For millennia, babies of all colors and cultures slept with their parents. In fact, to survive, there was no other choice. When homes consisted of one room, parents weren't exactly going to leave their little one outside the door as a tempting midnight snack for predators. But enter the "modern era," complete with infant formula and a few wise guys. Now we're in a whole new ballgame. The mindset of Western industrialized societies shifted, leading us to wrongly think that solitary infant sleep was "normal" and ideal. Paired with the warning not to spoil babies, the cry-it-out approach to baby nighttime "soothing" emerged.

Today's mamas have an avalanche of expert rulebooks urging them to let their babies cry: Benjamin Spock's *Baby and Child Care*, T. Berry Brazelton's *Touchpoints*, Burton L. White's *The New First Three Years of Life,* Arlene Eisenberg's *What to Expect the First Year*, *Solve Your Child's Sleep Problems* by Dr. Richard Ferber, and Gary Ezzo's *On Becoming Baby Wise*. Authors' suggestions vary, but their bottom line is that babies sleep differently than adults, which upsets parents' way of life. These authors urge us to reclaim sleep for mom and dad by training babies to adopt adult sleep habits after about four to five months of age.

While we can relate to those who crave a return to our pre-baby sleep routine, bedtime changes no matter how we handle it. Some babies respond to sleep training; others do not. We are surprised, however, that these experts shifted public views on babies' needs based on opinion, not science. We'll share the research to make sure you get the whole picture.

Backpedaling on Sleep Training

Most of us have seen the books endorsing solo sleep, tears and all, but few know their authors had second thoughts. In the 1979 Redbook article "What parents told me about handling children's sleep problems," Dr. T. Berry Brazelton wrote,

> *When I advised against bringing children into their parents' bed in an earlier article, I received many letters from parents who felt that sleeping alone is a custom our society unreasonably demands of its small children. I was impressed and have learned a great deal from the letters that expressed this point of view. I hadn't realized how many parents did NOT believe in helping a child learn to sleep alone at night. Their letters and their arguments made me reevaluate my...rigid ideas on handling sleep problems in our culture.*

We can't forget Dr. Ferber, who is known in different circles as either the wisest man on earth, or a cold-hearted baby trainer. (We suspect, like the rest of us, he falls somewhere in the middle.) His 1986 book warned parents that bringing babies into bed, except for the occasional night during illness, was a bad idea. He said that sleeping alone was necessary for kids to become autonomous adults.

But in a 1999 New Yorker article, "Sleeping With the Baby," Ferber recanted, too. "'I wish I hadn't written those sentences…That came out of some of the existing literature. It is a blanket statement that is just not right. There are plenty of examples of co-sleeping where it works out just fine. My feeling now is that children can sleep with or without their parents. What's really important is that the parents work out what they want to do."

Trends come and go. In the early 1900s, cocaine was thought to be a miracle cure for many ailments. So let's not jump on the latest sleep bandwagon before we've covered the facts. Brazelton and Ferber would likely agree.

How Babies Sleep

Discrepancies between how babies actually sleep and how the public believes they should sleep mean bad news for babies. We'll break down the back-story on each.

Soaring Expectations

There's no shortage of literature telling mothers when their babies "should" sleep through the night. Experts can't even agree on what sleeping through the night means, never mind when it should happen. Sleeping through the night is usually defined as an uninterrupted five-hour stretch. Some say it can happen when a baby reaches 13 pounds. Some advise parents to wait six months before you try to "help" them. Author Suzy Giordano believes your angel baby should be at *Twelve Hours' Sleep by Twelve Weeks Old. On Becoming Baby Wise* ups the ante, expecting a full night's uninterrupted sleep at just eight weeks!

Around three months, those Babycenter.com emails suggest your infant should be settling into a nice pattern of six to eight-hour stretches. While we've met some babies for whom this was true, it's almost always a phase. The expectation that babies sleep like adults before they're developmentally ready is all too common in our culture. The idea developed when bottle-fed cow's milk was trendy. Cow's milk has bigger molecules, more fat and less sugar than human milk, and is designed for growth best suited to, say, cows. Cow's milk (now formula) promotes more sleep in infants because it keeps them full for longer between feeds. You're probably thinking, "Yeah…and?" While it's nice for parents, the question is, how good is it for human babies?

Our utopian vision of babies who sleep through the night doesn't jive with the findings of biocultural anthropologist and breastfeeding expert Kathy Dettwyler:

> Human children are designed to be sleeping with their parents. The sense of touch is the most important sense to primates, along with sight. The expected pattern is for mother and child to sleep together, and for child to be able to nurse whenever they want during the night. Normal, healthy, breastfed and co-sleeping children do not sleep "through the night" (say 7-9 hours at a stretch) until they are 3-4 years old, and no longer need night nursing. I repeat—this is normal and healthy.[3]

THE SCOOP ON SELF-SOOTHING

You've probably heard the buzz about self-soothing. It's the most cited motivation for letting babies cry in their cribs. Well-intentioned parents want to give their infants the best, including an opportunity to develop into strong, independent people! If mom and dad cuddle and hold their little ones while they sleep, don't babies get the wrong message? Actually, research shows cuddles send the *right* message: the ability to self-soothe is learned by observing others, rather than figuring it out blindly.[4]

Think of it this way. If you weren't taught to swim, and were thrown in the middle of the ocean, do you think you'd learn the crawl? You may learn to tread water, but eventually you'd drown. We learn to swim by watching others carefully, and practicing with those who already know how to swim.

Self-soothing works the same way. Babies drink up parental love and cuddles on their way to sleep. When nurtured at night, they learn that sleep is a safe, peaceful time. Once they are developmentally ready, children put themselves to bed the way mom and dad did.[5] There's a scientific name for this: guided learning. But most mamas just call it intuitive parenting.

Kelly Bonyata, IBCLC and founder of KellyMom, comments:

Your baby will begin to comfort herself and to sleep for longer stretches at her own developmental pace. If your baby wants to nurse at night, it is because she does need this, whether it's because she is hungry or because she wants to be close to mom. Sleeping through the night is a developmental milestone that your baby will reach when she is ready. Trying to force baby to reach this before her time may result in other problems later on.

Ready for more proof that eight hours isn't the end-all-be-all? There's a good deal of evidence that the eight-hour sleep stretch is a modern invention! Roger Elrick's book *At Day's Close: A History of Nighttime*, shows we're built to sleep in two distinct sleep chunks, with a period of wakefulness in the middle. So when your baby doesn't want to go back to bed in the middle of the night, and you've ruled out the usual suspects, you may want to just chalk it up to physiology.

Sleeping Like a Baby

Just what do babies' sleep habits look like? First, they have shorter sleep cycles than adults: about half as long, lasting just 50 minutes. A sleep cycle is the total time spent in active (light) and deep stages of sleep. Adults have four periods of active sleep on an average night. Babies have twice as many. That means a baby is vulnerable to waking about eight times a night (and some do!). If he's hungry, wet, cold, or just missing mama, a baby may fully arouse during these times. Such short sleep cycles may seem inconvenient to parents, but they're actually a protective mechanism, especially during the early months. A baby who sleeps too deeply might not wake up when it's time for him to eat, or if he's having trouble breathing.

The way babies enter sleep is also different from adults. If you've ever held a sleeping newborn in your arms, you may recognize the stages. Instead of heading directly into deep sleep like adults, babies go into an active sleep for about 20 minutes. Then, there's a 10-minute transition period, the lightest sleep of the cycle, followed by about 20 minutes of deep sleep. His sleep stage explains why moving a sleeping baby sometimes wakes him up, and other times doesn't affect him in the least. It's all timing.

There's no quick switch to bring us from infant to adult sleep habits. Around six months, babies begin to enter deep sleep for longer periods of time, and their cycles gradually mature. But it's not until age four that his sleep cycles start to look like ours!

Like Bonyata said, trying to force your baby to sleep deeply for long stretches may work, but evidence shows that deep sleep isn't always in their best interest. Babies are born with only a quarter of their full brain size, and by age three the brain is almost its adult size. When does the brain do all of its growing? It develops and synthesizes information during active sleep.[6,7,8]

So let's give our babies—and ourselves—a break from unrealistically high expectations. Twelve hours a night would be a nice treat, but understanding what's going on inside that little head may give us just an ounce more patience, and a smidge more motivation to keep on keepin' on. Plus, before we know it, we'll be struggling to drag them out of bed!

Sleep Tips to Lean On

Co-sleeping doesn't guarantee a solid night's sleep, even if your little one is just a breath away. When your baby's going through an extended sleep strike, it can be hard to know up from down. It's often during a sleep deprived, desperate moment that mamas are willing to try anything to get their babies to sleep—including letting them cry 'til they conk. What *is* a mom to do when she needs to prop her lids open to get through the day, but doesn't want her little one to shed unnecessary tears?

An ounce of prevention. Give your little one plenty of opportunity to work out his jiggles, whether he's crawling, walking, or playing. Daylight regulates our sleep cycles, so enjoy a walk, trip to the park, or jaunt around the backyard. And remember, babies often need more time to transition than we do. So the last hours before bed should be a gentle wind-down, rather than a time to romp around the house with loud noises and bright lights.

A winning routine. As with other baby-friendly practices, reading your little one's cues is foremost. It's usually pretty clear when babies are tired. Their eyes look heavy or darker, they yawn, and they fuss. If you wait too long to get them down though, you may miss your window and end up with an over-tired baby on your hands. You don't have to read the exact same story, and play the exact same song, at exactly 7pm every night. But a routine that takes into account your baby's sleep signals can help him know what comes next. A bath, books, massage and milk are star players in many parents' bedtime routines.

Carrier to the rescue. What about that sweet little guy who asserts his desire to stay up and hang with mom? This can be frustrating, especially when you *know* your little one needs some shut-eye. Take a deep breath. He'll fall asleep eventually. Are you putting him to sleep on his own? Most babies prefer to fall asleep while nursing, or in their mother's arms.

When they're very young, a carrier or wrap can mimic mamas embrace. As they get older, you can lie next to them in bed and nurse or pat their back, and sneak away when you're sure they're out for good. Either way, a change of scenery is often very helpful. Strap on a wrap, head outdoors, and feel him melt in your arms.

It takes two. Is your baby waking every time you put him down? If he's your first, consider napping (or heading to bed early) with him. *But you have so much to do!* A well-rested mama is more productive and responsive than her sleep-deprived peers. If you're jonesin' to make a cup of tea, and have a little "me" time, try nursing to sleep (or patting to sleep) while lying down on a safe surface, like a crib or full-sized mattress on the floor. That way, you don't have to transfer a sleeping baby and you may be able to take a few precious moments for yourself.

Cat-nap syndrome. Just when you've settled into your book, dinner recipe, or email…he's up. Some babies have trouble making it through the transition part of their sleep cycle. They're missing mama, hungry, cold, hot, or have to go pee. Don't give up too easily though! Once you rule out hunger, temperature, and potty breaks, you may find that if you snuggle up for a few minutes, your baby will settle down again.

Back in the sack. Babies who are sick, teething, going through a growth spurt, or hitting developmental milestones like rolling over, crawling, or walking, tend to have wonky sleep schedules. (And if you know anything about babies, you know this can happen every other week…) If your baby falls into one of these categories, fear not. This too shall pass.

But what if he has all his teeth, he's walking, and he still wants to party like it's 1999 in the middle of the night? Ultimately it'll take some trial and error to find what works for your family, but you may want to try some combo of the following.

- A walk around the block (or the house) in the carrier, or a bounce on the exercise ball
- A few sips of water calms some babies
- Keep lights low to maintain high melatonin levels
- Singing in a soft voice
- White noise can be soothing when falling asleep, and helps some babies stay asleep longer
- Lightly running your fingers across his eyebrows, forehead, or up and down his cheeks, arms, or legs

- Lie down next to your baby and take slow, loud, deep breaths—the sound and the sensation of your belly rising and falling may lull him into relaxation

If your baby spends part of his night sad and crying in your arms, keep in mind that venting frustration in the security of your arms is a far different situation than leaving your baby in a crib to "self-soothe."

Overheard…

Before our daughter was born, we thought she'd sleep in the crib all the time. But we changed our minds on her first night home—she woke every time I put her in the bassinet after a feeding, but slept soundly when we brought her into our bed. We learned that the baby also gets a vote.

~Debbie, mom to Natalie

I'm Not Doing That Because…

Before we dive into why we love bringing our babies into bed, let's do some myth busting.

My baby will never leave the bed! This is often parents' biggest fear. Megan, Mark, and Anabella were briefly featured in CNN's 2011 "Extreme Parenting" series about co-sleeping, and at the end of the segment Kyra Phillips, the news anchor, mused, "I've never seen that end well." Her words reflected one of our society's most persistent myths—if we "spoil" our kids by letting them sleep close to us, they'll never learn to be independent.

We seldom stop to ask if it's in our best interest to raise independent infants. There are absolutely no studies showing that independence in infancy translates into independence in adulthood. And while some will lead you to believe that if you respond to your baby immediately he'll be forever clingy, there's no research to prove that, either.

In fact, studies have found just the opposite.

Parenting pioneers John Bowlby and Mary Ainsworth found that babies who are given love, nourishment and proximity early in life trust their caregivers and feel safe enough to explore on their own. On the flip side, babies who can't depend on consistent responsiveness tend to be clingy and insecure as toddlers.

Psychology professor Darcia Narvaez conducted three studies in 2010, all of which found infancy and early childhood a critical time for developing morals and social skills.[9] Narvaez identified seven areas in which parenting can support babies' growth into compassionate adults: touch—carrying your baby close; responsivity—responding to cries promptly; breastfeeding for at least two to five years; sleeping in close proximity to parents; maintaining close relationships with adults; playing with kids of different ages; and enjoying social support in a close community. Children who grew up in a community that valued these practices had better mental health, empathy and moral conscience, and higher IQs.

It's a bad habit. Ironically, Dr. Spock, Dr. Brazelton, and Dr. Ferber all insisted babies sleep in a separate room to prevent negative habits and sleep disorders. However, these men lumped together conscious co-sleeping—a nurturing, pro-active practice of bunking with your baby from birth, with stopgap co-sleeping—a reactive habit of letting older children hop in to solve impromptu sleep problems.

Overheard...

I co-slept until age four. I felt very close to my mom as a child, but was also quite independent. Interestingly, out of all my siblings I'm the most outgoing and independent, and I'm the only one who co-slept. I've grown into a successful adult despite my "habit"! I even enjoy being alone.

I like to think that my sons and I chose to co-sleep. I was open to it, and that's what they wanted to do. There's no denying they sleep best with mom and dad. I love feeling them next to me in the middle of the night, and I love waking up to their smiling faces in the morning.

I co-sleep because I enjoy it, but I also believe it'll lay the foundation for confident, well-adjusted adults.

~Aimie, mom to William and Andrew

While allowing a child to naturally wean himself from the family bed (yes, it will happen!) generally leads to a healthy sleeper, children who have been in their own bed from day one often exhibit disturbing behaviors or habits that are considered "normal" in our culture. Dr. Ferber's *Solve Your Child's Sleep Habits* has a chapter titled,

"Headbanging, body rocking, and head rolling." Yes, really. Many parents shrug off these behaviors because they're common, assuming they're developmentally normal issues.

But peoples who traditionally co-sleep are shocked to learn of these behaviors in our children. Deborah Jackson, author of *Three in a Bed*, comments, "In another cultural context, this book might be titled *Create Your Child's Sleep Problems.* When we decide to sleep-train our babies and they protest, we then need whole books reassuring us about the normality of their self-harming behaviors."

*But the media says…*Television, magazines, and the radio all have a field day with co-sleeping deaths. There's more than enough programming out there to make you want to put your child in another room and lock the door. Because of negative publicity, people worry about safety. It's important, however, to keep in mind the two greatest risk factors—extreme poverty and stressful circumstances, including abuse and marital or relational strife. Obesity, drugs, alcohol, smoking, and unsafe bedding place babies at risk too. However, a much higher percentage of infants die in solitary sleep than those sharing sleep in an environment where those risk factors aren't present.

Scientific evidence—and common sense—agrees: bed-sharing itself isn't dangerous; rather it's how it's done that is.[10] That doesn't make for a great headline, though.

In a sweeping statement, the U.S. Consumer Product Safety Commission (CPSC) issued a 1999 warning against babies sleeping in adult beds. The statement was based on a study of 2,178 death reports of newborns to age two in a seven-year period, from 1990 to 1997.[11] What the CPSC warning did not include was parallel data on the 2,991 infants who died of SIDS in 1997 alone.[12] Yes, that one-year SIDS figure is greater than the number of babies who died over the course of seven years while co-sleeping, including those napping on couches—which is a big no-no, by the way!

The majority of the SIDS deaths were babies who were alone in their cribs. Sadly, about 2,500 babies continue to die of SIDS every year.[13] They failed to mention that though every death is a tragedy, the statistical significance of about 64 deaths per year out of almost 4 million live births is actually very low.

The CPSC dropped the ball. They had a chance to educate us about safe bed-sharing, and they didn't. So now, we co-sleepers are the notorious bootleggers and rumrunners of the bed-sharing prohibition. Our national co-sleeping ignorance leads to tragedies like suffocation on couches or waterbeds. Many deaths in adult beds are due to bed frames, or gaps between mattresses or furniture, which babies slip into, and then asphyxiate. If parents were given some basic information, they could easily make adjustments to create a safe co-sleeping environment, and avoid tragedy.

No one else is doing it. Take the media vilification of co-sleeping, add some uninformed nurses and doctors, and sprinkle on incredulity from relatives and social circles—it's no wonder many families are "closet co-sleepers." No one wants to be socially ostracized. But, odds are, you wouldn't be the first of your friends to co-sleep. Though there's no easy way to know exactly how many parents snuggle all night with their little one, various sources point to a co-sleeping rate anywhere from 40–70%!

You'll never have sex. If you think the bed is the only place lovemaking can happen, get creative. Isn't that how the best sex happens, anyway?

Overheard...

In the early years we resorted many times to the guest room or the couch. With our last baby we upgraded to a king bed so we stay in bed most of the time, though there were a few times when the shaking woke the baby.

~Jennifer, mom to Tamara, Alex, Megan and Kiera

Benefits of Co-Sleeping

Now for the fun part. Here's where we get to tell you why we love co-sleeping. Sharing a sleep space with your baby has so many benefits that people have written entire books about it. We strongly encourage you to read one or two of them. (We shared our favorites in the Resources section at the end of this book.) Hearing from well-researched enthusiasts boosts your co-sleeping confidence and gives you a feel-good community that has successfully shared sleep.

Babies sleep better! You know those scenes we're primed to expect as new parents? The one where we're up all night, rocking our baby to sleep, dark circles under our eyes? Those images are straight out of the separate sleeping handbook! Yes, some co-sleeping babies have trouble falling or staying asleep, but generally the reason babies cry so much at night is that they're not used to being alone. By recreating a nurturing womb-like environment, with your baby snuggled up next to you, you'll banish most of those stereotypical sleepless nights.

> **Overheard...**
>
> *Dalia had a really hard time falling asleep by herself in the early weeks. No matter how easily she fell asleep in my arms, she would inevitably awaken when I tried to put her back in her bassinet. Misha and I took turns, sleep deprived, bouncing her in our arms, swaddling and unswaddling her, singing to her, anything we could think of. Anything but bed sharing, which our nurse warned us was dangerous, and we didn't even consider as an option.*
>
> *Our perspective on bed sharing began to shift when we met co-sleeping families. After thorough Internet research on the dangers of co-sleeping, I compiled a safety checklist and tried it the next night. We were so nervous; I barely slept that night. I was terrified I'd roll over onto her. I slept a bit better with each passing night until we had successfully slept a full night together, waking just slightly to latch her on.*
>
> *Co-sleeping is one of the things we both love most about parenting. What began as a stopgap solution to sleepless nights is now a treasured family tradition.*
>
> *~Miriam, mom to Dalia*

Less stress. Cortisol, the stress hormone, is lower in mothers and babies who co-sleep. Low levels of cortisol are important for a baby's healthy development, since cortisol distracts his energy from his day job—growing.[14]

No more tears. A baby who knows his mother is close by has little reason to cry at night. Research studies show he has fewer reasons to cry during the day, too.[15]

Tips to Prevent SIDS

By James McKenna, PhD, Director, University of Notre Dame Mother-Baby Behavioral Sleep Laboratory; author of Sleeping with Your Baby.

Close maternal-infant sleep proximity has a strong protective benefit against SIDS.[16,17] Human infants are not designed to sleep alone, as they are born exceedingly neurologically immature. Their bodies don't easily absorb or maximally benefit by drinking the milk of another species (cows) lacking in specific human antibodies. The best protection you can give your baby is to never let your baby sleep alone, despite the American Academy of Pediatrics' recommendation. In addition to sleeping near your baby, breastfeeding exclusively for at least the first few months has a strong protective effect against SIDS.

If you're not breastfeeding, separate surface co-sleeping (bassinet or crib next to bed) is more appropriate.

Practically speaking, always place your baby to sleep on his back. But remember—safe infant sleep begins before your baby is born. Never smoke during your pregnancy: ingested and absorbed smoke by your fetus injures the very brain tissues and cells responsible for arousing and oxygenating during sleep. Babies need those tissues and cells to effectively terminate prolonged breathing pauses that may be responsible for SIDS.

As our scientific studies show, co-sleeping/nursing babies exhibit more species-normal infant sleep, which is less time spent in deep sleep. This makes it easier for them to arouse to terminate apneas (breathing pauses) and is simply the way the human infant feeding, sleep and breathing system was designed to most optimally function, increasing the chances of healthy development and survival.

Survival. Babies who sleep close to their mothers have more stable temperatures, heart rhythms, and breathing patterns.[18] During the early months, it's not just a benefit—it's survival. To put it plainly, bottle-feeding and solitary sleep increase a baby's risk of SIDS.[19]

Breastfeeding is a breeze. As we discussed earlier, nighttime nursing is a normal, healthy habit. Compared to formula, mother's milk is low in protein and fat and has a high lactose content, which is great for immature digestive systems, but also means that babies are hungry often. "Training" babies to sleep by themselves, without access to food, is biologically unnatural. (It's important to note that formula fed babies often sleep longer stretches because they are fuller longer. That IS normal for them!)

Sleeping in close quarters with your baby makes these midnight feasts easier. If he shares your bed, you might even find you don't wake up when he latches on! For moms with low milk supply, or those who are working outside the home, sharing sleep is a feel-good way to boost supply, too.

> **Overheard...**
>
> *In the early weeks, my baby slept in a bassinet. I nursed him in a rocker then transferred him as gently as possible. Then my friend mentioned nursing while lying down. I tried it and fell in love! I fell asleep a couple times while he was nursing and we ended up sleeping next to each other in my bed.*
>
> *I had heard and read that this was a dangerous thing to do, and felt so guilty. Then, I went to a mom's group and found that several other mothers regularly co-slept with their babies. It was easier for me; he slept better and rarely cried, knowing I was so close.*
>
> *~Jen, mom to Connor*

More confident kids. A growing body of research touts the psychological perks of cosleeping. Findings are impressive. Co-sleeping babies grow into adults with higher self-esteem, greater satisfaction with life, a more affectionate demeanor and fewer psychological issues.[20]

Natural child spacing. Co-sleeping can be a natural way to assist child spacing. As we mentioned in Milk, frequent suckling at the breast delays ovulation, so nighttime snacking may keep your flow at bay. Once the baby starts sleeping for longer chunks, and nursing frequency goes down, your period may return.

Hugs and kisses. Nighttime parenting is generally a sweet, intimate time. Drowsy babies are eager for touch and cuddles, and often drift back to sleep easily (barring teething, colds and developmental milestones). And we'd be hard pressed to give up seeing those early smiles as our babies wink and blink their way into morning.

Overheard...

I can't describe how at peace I feel knowing that my daughter is curled up next to me, warm, safe and content.

~Bethany, mom to Sadie

Co-Sleeping Snapshot

We don't want to give you recipes for sharing sleep with your baby; we want to give you ideas. Every culture and every family has a different method that works for them. But in Western society, where sharing sleep is so taboo, you might not know what co-sleeping looks like (we didn't!). We'll share some examples, but please don't take them as gospel. What feels right for your family is best.

We're going to state the obvious again: co-sleeping safety is top priority. Needless injuries and deaths have resulted from dangerous environments. If you bring your baby into bed, please internalize and implement the guidelines for sleep safety.

Side-car co-sleepers. Dr. McKenna recommends the Arm's Reach brand co-sleeper. It's called a "side-car co-sleeper" because it attaches to your bed using a tether that fits between the box spring and mattress. If you're nervous about taking your baby into bed, or your bed seems too small, a co-sleeper is a very good option. It can be invaluable for naps, and when the baby is ready for night-night, but you're not! As soon as your little one figures out how to pull up on the sides, though, you'll need a new plan.

It's important to note that the sleeping surface of the co-sleeper is, by design, not level with your bed. So, if you've had a C-section, or are just plain exhausted, be aware that you'll be leaning over and lifting your baby a few inches in and out of the co-sleeper. Some moms like that the baby has his own space, but that means...the baby has his own space. There's no cuddling or easy flipping for a quick snack in the middle of the night: you have to be semi-awake to nurse.

Free-standing bassinets or cribs. Some nights with your baby in bed are less comfortable than others. Like anything else, co-sleeping isn't a wonderful, blissful experience *all of the time.* You may get a foot in the ribs; your arm may lose feeling because the baby's head is resting on it; or the little noises of your precious newborn may be distracting. For most co-sleeping families, these are small inconveniences compared to the benefits of sharing sleep. However, a free-standing portable crib, such as a bassinet or a traditional crib placed near your bed, may be an option if you feel it would be best for baby to have his own space.

Moms who are formula feeding may want to choose this option as well, especially in the early days. Breastfeeding mothers, due to hormones, are most in tune with their babies. Compared to bottle feeders, they tend to move babies to safer positions, including on their back, away from pillows. Breastfeeding mothers are also more likely to position themselves in ways that prevent overlaying.[21]

In bed. Whether it's because they fall asleep while nursing, or because they love snuggling with their baby, some moms bring their little one right into the bed. There are a variety of ways to hold your baby, but the most popular seems to be mom lying on her side with her bottom arm cradling her little one, and her knees tucked up underneath the baby. This position is a safeguard against overlaying, and is most common among breastfeeding mothers. Newborns are like heat-seeking missiles and don't normally roll away from the warmth of their mother, but nonetheless, the baby is held secure in this position.

Some moms snuggle their baby while nursing, and then unlatch and turn on their backs or stomachs after a feed. Others hold the baby in the crook of their arm all night. Most find it helpful to tuck a pillow between their knees and one behind their backs for support, as well.

If you think you have to be a gymnast to maneuver a drowsy, hungry baby to the other breast in the middle of the night, don't worry! You can actually feed from both breasts while lying on one side, by further angling your torso toward your baby. It takes some practice to get the hang of it, as does side-lying nursing, but soon becomes second nature.

Safety in the Sack

By now we've driven home that how you share sleep with your baby is of utmost importance. Let's get down to the nitty gritty, though. Understanding the ins and outs of co-sleeping spells safety.

Firm up. Sadly, your favorite waterbed, pillow top, or memory foam mattress that molds to your body isn't best for the baby. Your little one may sink in and have his airways obstructed. A firm natural latex or organic cotton mattress provides great support, without the risk (and toxic fumes!).

Get off the couch. Couches are nice to snuggle up with your honey, but are notoriously dangerous spots to snooze with the baby. Nodding off into a deep sleep—especially as an exhausted new parent—poses a big risk for babies, who can roll into crevices or onto the floor.

No smoking. According to a 2008 CDC study, one in five Americans over age eighteen smokes.[22] We won't share the risks of smoking, as you'd have to live in a cave to not know, but we will say that smoking and sharing sleep don't mix. Smoking lowers levels of prolactin, reducing a mom's awareness of her baby's needs.

Sober up. Find a new space for the baby if you or your partner is under the influence of alcohol, drugs, or any judgment-impairing substance. This goes for medications that have the ability to alter your physical or mental state. These substances increase the risk of overlaying.

Lighten your load. Heavy comforters, extra pillows, and thick blankets all pose risks, since little ones (even newborns), can be quite the wigglers. We don't want them to find their way under the bedding and risk suffocation. You can either turn up the heat (not too warm!), wear an extra layer and put the baby in a sleep sack, or use a blanket tucked in at your waist level. Co-sleeping babies are often hotter than their cribbing counterparts, so take it easy on the layers until you're familiar with your baby's clothing needs. Mom's body gives off so much heat that summer babies are usually fine in their birthday suits.

Megan, A Novel Mama

A Sleep Story

When I was pregnant, I knew I wanted to breastfeed. I wasn't sure I wanted to lose sleep over it though. I had visions of wearing the hall rug threadbare, pacing from our room to a pastel colored nursery. And then, I read that some moms put cribs in their room, and it seemed like the perfect solution. So, I ditched the Pottery Barn catalogs full of baby-room inspiration, and looked into organic mattresses, sustainably harvested wooden cribs, and natural bedding. My husband wanted to have me committed when I tallied up the bill for our baby's sleep situation. We could have rented her a room at the Ritz for the year at the same price.

I eventually settled on an Arm's Reach co-sleeper, so our new girl could be as close as possible. It wasn't that I was against a family bed. I never even considered it an option.

The first night in the hospital, I realized that an arm's reach was too far. I could hear Anabella breathing and squirming alone in the bassinet next to me, and after about ten minutes, I couldn't stand it. I brought her into my hospital bed, and she quickly fell asleep on my chest. Hours later the nurse on duty scolded me. Didn't I know how dangerous that was?

I did. Our families made it abundantly clear through emailed web links, clipped articles, and casual phone conversations. My father saw negative media on co-sleeping. My mother and sister were concerned I'd have a five year old in bed, and wouldn't be able to "get her out."

But my college degree paid off—I knew there was more to the co-sleeping story than the media cared to tell. I did my research, busting myths about co-sleeping, and felt confident the benefits outweighed the risks.

Anabella spent her first year (and beyond!) in our bed, and though our families weren't convinced, they didn't need to be. We made our own best decision. As for the Arm's Reach—it became a laundry drying rack, a toy bin, and later, an overnight pottying station. For the next baby, we'll skip the "stuff" and bring him right into bed.

Less is more. Especially in the early months, a baby is usually safest between mom and a mesh bed rail. Fathers and especially older siblings generally don't have the same sensitivity to a new baby in bed. And please, find Fido a new sleep space. Dogs and cats are particularly ill-suited co-sleepers for baby.

Say no to cracks. Check your bed thoroughly for spots where the baby could get lodged. If your mattress sits apart from the headboard, side rails or wall, be sure it's snugly secured before your baby joins you.

When three's a crowd. If either parent is overweight or obese, take caution to investigate any dips or crevices that a baby could roll into. When in doubt, keep baby out.

Go austere. Jewelry, pajamas with fringes and strings, and perfume all may interfere with safe sleeping. Use common sense. A pair of stud earrings you wear every day is likely harmless, but Chanel N°5 can assault your baby's delicate breathing faculties.

Greening your Bedroom

Safe bed-sharing is just one piece of creating a baby's best sleep environment. Healthy mattresses, bed sheets, and even PJs are an important part of keeping your little one safe while catching zzz's.

Mattresses

We spend one-third of our life sleeping (if we're lucky!), so our mattress should be a good one! But we've been led to think that the best mattress is simply the most comfortable.

Unlike food, mattress labels are rarely read for "ingredients," and polyurethane foam seldom raises any red flags, despite being a skin and respiratory irritant. Formaldehyde and other highly toxic glues are used as adhesives to hold the mattress parts together.[23] Our skin is exposed to the top layer of the mattress for eight hours a day. And if you're on a conventional mattress, that means you're skin-to-skin with pesticides and flame-retardants. Neither group wins awards for their health benefits.

The good news is that there are some healthy sleeping options. Safe, non-toxic mattresses are becoming more widely available and are increasingly becoming more affordable.

Have you heard of 100% natural latex? It's hypo-allergenic, anti-microbial, and dust mite resistant. If that isn't enticing enough, it's actually really comfortable. An added bonus is that latex is pretty firm, allowing far less transfer of motion, so your mattress won't squeak and bounce if you go to bed later than your baby. Natural latex from the rubber tree is the healthiest way to go. While 100% natural latex will off-gas, its gasses come from natural materials, whereas synthetic latex off-gasses toxic chemicals.

If natural latex doesn't appeal, try an organic cotton mattress. Global Organic Textile Standard (GOTS) requires that all mattress parts, including fire retardants, meet strict non-toxic requirements.

And remember, companies can use almost any adjective they want to sell these products. "Natural" may not mean what you think. Bamboo is a good example. It's a fast-growing plant, but most manufacturers use toxic chemicals to process it into sheets or fabric.

If buying a new bed isn't in your budget, consider an organic mattress pad to put a layer of natural fiber between you and your mattress. Be sure that whatever mattress or topper you choose is relatively firm; the less plush the better. You want to make sure that a baby who rolls over in bed has clear access to his airways.

Flame Retardants

Picture it: your house is on fire. Flames are moving toward the room where your baby is sleeping. You start to panic, then breathe a sigh of relief—the baby is wearing non-flammable pajamas. Ridiculous, right? So why are we pumping toxins into our baby items?

You'll find flame retardant chemicals in polyurethane foam-based products because of an outdated flammability standard in the state of California called TB 117. Since manufacturers aren't shipping separate products to California, they protect their bottom line by pumping all their products with cheap flame-retardants. TB 117 doesn't specifically state that chemicals are necessary, but chemicals happen to be the cheapest and easiest way to meet the standard.

Of 101 products in a 2011 study of baby products (nursing pillows, car seats, changing table pads, sleep positioners, infant carriers and strollers, high chairs, nursery rocking chairs/gliders, etc.) 80 tested positive for one or more types of chemical flame retardant. [24] They don't just slow down flames, though; they're toxic. Think lowered IQ, reproductive problems, difficulty becoming pregnant, poor sperm quality, hormone disruption, and cancer.[25]

We can protect our little ones—and ourselves—but it may take some effort. Keep your eyes out for items made from wool, cotton, polyester, or down, (not polyurethane foam), which are not generally treated with flame retardant chemicals. Check the baby's PJs to make sure they don't say "flame-resistant."

Cotton in the Sack

Much of our bedding and clothing is made from cotton. Cotton plants attract many insects, so they need pest control. But does pest management have to harm humans? Once we know the suffix -cide in Latin means *kill, killer, murder,* or *to cause death,* words like herbicide, insecticide, fungicide, and pesticide are easily translated. These "killers" end up in our water supply, our food, and our bodies. Conventional cotton farming may be cheaper, but our health, planet and cotton farmers pay a hefty price.

Organic cotton can get pricy, so how does one balance health and budget? Our rule of thumb when buying cotton: consider how many hours the baby will be exposed to a given item. Bed sheets and PJ's tend to top the charts with our babies.

Miriam's Coaching Corner

Gratitude

Sharing your bed with a baby is a big adjustment. Not only are babies' sleep rhythms different than ours, relationship dynamics inevitably change as the family expands. It's easy to take your partner for granted in the early days of parenthood, as stress runs high and sleep deprivation magnifies emotions. But when we take the time to appreciate each other, we create the space to recognize and celebrate the very magical changes taking place in our lives.

Pillow Talk. *When you turn out the lights, take a few moments to express your gratitude for your partner's qualities or actions that you appreciate. You may choose to share three items, starting the sentence with, "I'm grateful for..."*
    It's amazing how much having this brief conversation can shift the dynamics of your days—and of your relationship. You may find yourself looking forward to it every night!

Sleep Tight

A good night's sleep is the most precious thing during that crucial first year, both for our babies and for ourselves. And when we sleep in a way that is line with our babies' needs, including safety, nourishment and access to loving caretakers, we set up the whole family for more peace at night. Proximity is one of the best gifts we can give ourselves and our little ones to ensure quick and easy nighttime parenting. If you or your sleep space doesn't meet the safety standards, be sure to provide a separate sleeping option for your baby. Otherwise, snuggle up and enjoy each other! Sweet dreams.

Potty
respond to elimination needs

Babies and diapers. They go together like peanut butter and jelly; like Bert and Ernie; like peas in a pod. The ubiquitous "diaper cake" often showcases as a centerpiece at baby showers, and the big diapering question for expecting parents is "cloth or disposable?" We rarely hear of other options.

But around the world in Europe, North America, Australia and South Africa, pockets of in-the-know parents are embracing a third option. In some societies, this practice is so integral to the cultural fabric that it has no name. Westerners call it Elimination Communication (EC)[1], Infant Pottying or Natural Infant Hygiene.

You may have heard bits and pieces about "diaper-free babies." Don't worry. We're not going to ask you to skip diapers completely (unless you want to, of course). Infant pottying can be practiced full-time, part-time or occasionally, and creates an incredibly rewarding connection between caregivers and their baby. The practice itself is pretty straightforward—take the baby to a "toilet." Elimination Communication, its formal name, is most accurate, as communicating about babies' elimination needs is the crux of the practice.

We're all born with the instinct not to soil ourselves. Infants express their elimination needs the same way they communicate other bodily sensations, such as hunger and cold. They signal before elimination through a grimace, cry, squirm, or blank stare. Luckily, reading cues isn't rocket science. With determination and a little time, infant pottying can be a surprisingly enjoyable practice!

---

[1] While EC is a noun, practitioners also use it as a verb. *I am ECing my baby,* or *Yes, we EC.*

We'll provide all the details you'll need to get started ECing your baby, including hands-on advice and encouraging anecdotes from moms who have been there, done that. Like breastfeeding, you don't need anything, but many moms find it helpful to use diapers as a back up, so we'll prep you with important facts on cloth versus disposable to help you make an informed decision.

Why We Love EC

It's Easy to Be Green

Americans throw away 570 diapers per second. That's 49 million trashed diapers each day.

Guess where those single-use diapers end up? Landfills. In the U.S. alone, disposable diapers use up 100,000 tons of plastic and 800,000 tons of tree pulp annually. Alan Greene, author of *Raising Baby Green*, suggests the name "disposable diapers" is misleading, and represents clever marketing by the diaper industry. Diapers can't really be thrown away; they're just moved to another spot. Calling them "landfill" diapers, he suggests, is more accurate, given where they end up—and remain for 300–500 years.

Bonding with the Baby

If you've never communicated with your baby about his elimination habits, it's pretty hard to imagine how it might be a bonding experience. We assumed this perk was exaggerated before getting started, but soon proved ourselves wrong.

Moms who EC report fewer bouts of unexplained crying during their baby's first few months. Once we tune into our baby's elimination needs, we can identify and address them, just as we do with a hungry or tired baby. The benefit of anticipating and responding to your baby's needs is a huge motivator for many moms, and serves as a jumping off point for an even stronger relationship—and greater confidence in their new role as a mom.

Overheard...

About ten years before I had my daughter I read Nature's Children by Juliette de Bairacle Levy and it mentioned people who knew when their child had to go to the bathroom. I thought this type of intuition, communication, language or whatever it was sounded fantastic and magical. I wanted to know my child on this intimate level. I've learned that being able to anticipate and respond to Olive's potty cue is as valid as responding to her cues to eat or sleep.

~Maria, mom to Olive

Keeping in Touch

The most obvious benefit of offering the potty when a baby needs to go is for him to cultivate and maintain awareness of his elimination needs. He'll notice when his bladder is full and will squirm or cry out, letting mom know it's time to empty! Babies who use only diapers—especially disposables, where it's often hard to tell if they're wet—are taught to ignore their elimination needs, and have to re-learn body awareness when toilet training.

Babies who regularly have diaper-free time develop far less rashes. The reason is simple: diaper rash is a skin irritation usually caused by damp conditions, like a wet diaper. Other possible reasons for rash are bacteria or yeast. These perpetrators thrive in dark, damp places, like Junior's diaper. So understandably, lots of air and natural light will prevent rashes and speed up the healing of existing ones.

Why Doesn't Everyone Do It?

The short answer: we have a kind of collective PTSD. Early American potty training was so rigid that it scarred kids, leading Americans to throw the baby out with the chamber pot. The rest of the "civilized" world soon followed suit.

Early baby care "experts" (we use the term loosely because their advice was usually based on opinion, not science) knew that babies could use the toilet from birth. But they got carried away. Babies were strapped to toilets as soon as they could hold their heads up, and sticks of soap were inserted into baby bottoms to encourage regularity. Even worse, ugly toilet training tools like punishment and shame left tons of kids with emotional disturbances.

Western toileting took a major detour in the 1940s, as concerned U.S. baby care expert Dr. Benjamin Spock began recommending waiting until babies sat independently, around seven to nine months, to begin pottying. Later, Dr. Brazelton recommended parents look for seven "readiness" signs in their children, and not to begin toileting before all signs were present. Among his signs were the ability to say "no," bowel regularity and bodily awareness. In following his advice, parents effectively pushed their babies' pottying start dates to two or three years old.

How EC is Different

Given our recent past, it's easy to see why anything but a diapered baby is met with skepticism and even condemnation for parents "pushing" their children too quickly. But, as with co-sleeping, experts have failed to clarify the real issue. *How* you respond to your baby's elimination needs is entirely different than *when*.

We don't advocate turn-of-the-century tactics. In fact, we cringe when people comment that our little ones are "potty trained." We aim to understand their needs, and lay the foundation for a relationship of mutual respect. We're *communicating* with our babies, not *training* them. The difference may seem subtle (and possibly even irrelevant) before you start.

Let's draw a firmer boundary between traditional toilet training and potty-based communication. First and foremost, with EC there's no negativity around elimination. If your child arches his back when you put him on the potty, you're free to let him go—even if he pees in the corner, or in his diaper a moment later. Sometimes that's frustrating for mom, but it's counterproductive to obsess about the miss, shame the child or use any form of punishment.

EC philosophy inherently rejects all timelines as well. Babies are individuals, so assuming they should be at a given stage is detrimental to all involved. EC is about responding to your baby's needs—so have fun and relax. Otherwise, it's not worth doing!

Infant Pottying in India

By Laurie Boucke, author of Infant Potty Training

"I don't get it. How do they do it?" my friend Lisa asked me. We were walking along a dusty country road in India when a pick-up truck rolled past us. The back of the truck was packed with Sikh men, two small children and a woman. All of a sudden, one of the men took the baby in his arms, leaned him against his chest with the baby facing outward and made a sssshhhh sound. The baby boy peed over the back of the truck, somebody said "Shabash," ("Good!"), and he was passed to his mother.

"Amazing!" I said. No big deal for the Sikhs, but a miracle to us Westerners visiting India for the first time. Lisa and I were surprised to discover that babies in India don't wear diapers, and that they are toilet trained from about one month old.

The women we asked explained there are different ways of knowing. They use signals from the baby, timing or an intuitive feeling. One of the babies would crawl towards the bathroom when he had to go. One of the smaller ones would yell when he needed to go. The third baby didn't offer any clear signals, so his mother figured things out by using timing and intuition.

The women demonstrated over and over again that there is no need for diapers when raising a baby. Taking care of their children's toilet needs is viewed as an integral part of childcare. There is no squeamishness about it, and there was certainly never any complaining about it.

We were touched by the closeness between these mothers and babies. They communicated with each other on a level we had never seen before.

Around the World

In many societies throughout the globe, babies are pottied in response to their cues. In China, for example, cotton, water, and soap are all scarce items. Mothers make a whistling sound to cue their babies, and little ones dressed in split-crotch pants easily eliminate in response. By the time children can walk, around 12-14 months, they know to squat and eliminate on their own.

In many places throughout the globe, including India, Africa, Russia, and South America, locals use a similar method. In warmer climates, babies are carried naked in slings. Mothers respond to babies' cues and signals by taking the baby out of the sling, and little ones are free to eliminate without soiling themselves or their mamas.

So...What Now?

You want to start communicating with your little one about elimination, but you have no idea where to start. We didn't, either. Here are four tools to launch your EC relationship.

Get going. You can potty your baby from birth, or as early as you feel comfortable. Miriam got started soon after birth; Megan waited three months until they had settled into more of a routine. It's most important that pottying is enjoyable for everyone. If you're overly stressed by the idea, it's probably not the right time.

Read cues. It may seem hard to believe, but during his first few months, your little one probably communicates before he goes, whether you respond or not! Common signals include sudden fussing, squirming, grunting or crying out, becoming still, waking from sleep, or a specific facial expression.

Once your baby's old enough to notice visual cues, you may want to incorporate the sign for potty. Around six months—or earlier, if you'd like—you can show your baby the toilet sign every time you say potty. In American Sign Language, it looks like a closed fist, shaken from side to side, with your thumb peeking out between the index and middle finger.

Once a baby begins signing, it's pretty amazing to have him deliberately tell you that he needs to go. For some, this happens as early as nine months, but all babies develop and communicate at different rates and in different ways.

Miriam's Coaching Corner

Intuition

Our bodies are constantly sending us messages to keep us safe and help us thrive. Most of us aren't conscious of these messages, most of the time. But when the stakes are higher—we've all heard a story of someone who didn't get on a plane that ended up crashing—or when we're sizing up an unfamiliar situation, we often hear our inner voice. Intuition comes from a sensing or feeling space (heart or body), not a thinking space (mind).

Motherhood is an intensely emotional and bodily experience, so it's natural for intuition to kick in. Also, the stakes are incredibly high! We have another life depending on us. We need all the help we can get—and the best help comes from our own inner knowing. Intuition shows up differently in each of us. One of the best ways to build intuition is to get out of your head. For parents, that means being present with your baby.

Want to try an experiment?

Give your baby some diaper-free time. Tune in to him as fully as possible. Gaze at your baby intensely, noticing the tiniest details of his face or body. Let go of any ideas about what he needs. Open up to any insights that may arise.

Remember, intuition kicks in when the stakes are high. When the baby's got a bare booty, we Western moms are worried about having our fill-in-the-blank peed on. So when the baby's diaper comes off, our awareness tools kick into high gear.

The more you practice, the more you'll be able to distinguish which thoughts come from a place of fear, and which thoughts come from a place of inner knowing.

Not sure you can trust your gut? Give it a try. What do you have to lose? (Hint: if it's your heirloom rug, pick another room!)

Give cues. Around the world, mothers give their babies cues, like "ssshhh" or "psssss." In the early days of your EC journey, the cue is given when mom notices her baby going. Eventually, her baby associates the cue with relaxing his bladder and releases when he hears the sound.

Get support. In today's wired world, if none of your neighbors practice EC, you can still get all the help and encouragement you need online.

Pottying Intuition

When a mother from an EC-practicing culture was asked how she knew when her baby had to use the bathroom, she said, "How do you know when *you* have to go?" Just think about it. When you have to go to the bathroom, you know it because you feel it in your body. The sensation is unmistakable. In cultures where intuition is regularly drawn upon as a resource—as often, say, as we consult Google—the certainty of a baby's bodily needs is as solid as mom's own needs.

Caretakers who tune into their baby's elimination needs often experience the following types of intuition with their babies:

- An intense urge to pee (It may be your baby's!)
- A phantom pee: a warm sensation on your lap, as if you've been peed on (If you're dry, baby needs to go!)
- A sudden instinct or thought that it's potty time
- Just "knowing" that your baby needs to go.

Pottying Toolkit: The Basics

There are a variety of different holds and locations you can use to potty your baby. Parents generally call on several throughout the day, according to circumstances. Some babies don't mind nursing with a small bowl or potty under their bum. Others prefer you hold them over the sink after they've nursed. You'll quickly learn your baby's unique preferences.

Itty Bitty Baby

The easiest way to potty a tiny baby is to hold him facing outward with one hand under each thigh, his back pressed to your stomach, over the sink or toilet. Often by taking a deep breath, mom can signal her baby to relax and pee. When cueing the baby to poop, tense your stomach muscles against his back as a physical cue—a reminder to bear down and release his bowels. He may or may not go, but it's helpful for you to give him the opportunity.

Moms may hesitate to use the sink for fear of being unsanitary, but baby pee or breastfed baby poop is nothing a little water and vinegar can't handle. It literally all comes out in the wash.

Sitting Pretty

Once a baby gains some head and trunk control, he may enjoy being held upright over a small potty or sitting on your lap over a potty or bowl. After a few months, he'll be sitting on his own, handling toys or watching the world while perched on his pot.

If your baby immediately arches his back when you put him on the potty, it may be his way of telling you he's not interested. Sometimes, you may sense that he really does need to go but is unable to focus on the task in that moment. An older baby is often engrossed in what's going on around him, but may relax if given a toy, book, or sung a song. If he wants to get up, try again in a few minutes, but don't force him to stay. Pottying should be fun for everyone.

The Throne

Another option is to sit facing the back of a "real" toilet with your legs straddling either side. Let your baby sit on your lap, also facing the back of the toilet, while you hold under his thighs. It can be helpful to rest your forearms on your thighs and hold the baby slightly forward of your lap to avoid getting peed on. This position is particularly useful when pottying your baby in public restrooms!

The Dirt on Diapers

Most ECing parents use diapers as back up at least some of the time. So that leaves the decision: cloth or disposable ? For EC, we're partial to cloth, because the baby feels his wetness immediately. This physical reminder helps him maintain awareness of his bodily functions.

WHAT'S IN DISPOSABLE DIAPERS, ANYWAY?

Sadly, disposable diapers aren't just hurting the planet. Mass market 'sposies use bleach to make them white, releasing dioxins, which are found in trace amounts on disposable diapers. The WHO warns that dioxins can harm reproductive, immune, and endocrine systems.[1]

Disposable diapers have been linked with male infertility[2] and asthma! One study found several known respiratory irritants in the emissions from disposables. The study's authors concluded that disposable diapers should be considered as a cause or irritant in childhood asthma.[3]

While green companies like Seventh Generation, Earth's Best and Nature Babycare sell diapers without chlorine and fragrance, they still contain Sodium Polyacrylate (SAP), to absorb liquids. In 1985 SAP was removed from tampons because of a link to Toxic Shock Syndrome, a serious bacterial infection. Diaper makers tell us not to worry—the SAP never touches a baby's skin. But some mamas still find it too close for comfort.

That said, many parents who use cloth diapers supplement with disposables, especially when recovering from birth and adjusting to motherhood. If not practicing nighttime EC (more on that later) some parents use 'sposies overnight since many babies wet repeatedly, and some babies awaken fully when wet. For some parents, disposables may help keep your little one asleep.

Which Diaper is Greener?

Some people say the choice between cloth and disposables is a wash, so to speak, from an environmental perspective. This argument was birthed in a 2005 study by the UK's Environmental Agency that used the energy consumption of laundry machines manufactured in 1997 as a benchmark. They found that laundering 2.5 years of cloth diapers emitted 1,232 pounds of carbon dioxide equivalent, compared to 1,380 pounds of emissions from disposable diapers. As the many critics of this study have shown, today's appliances are much more energy efficient than those quoted in the study. Also, manufacturing disposable diapers uses 2.3 times more water than it takes to produce cloth diapers![4]

We're not just talking water, though. Those single use diapers generate 60 times more solid waste and use 20 times more crude oil and wood pulp than cloth diapers.[5] How about chlorine? Each disposable-diapered baby requires twenty pounds per year! Don't forget the 50 pounds of petroleum annually.[6] That's quite a resume for a tiny tot.

But you're using "natural" disposables that are "biodegradable?" Just because a diaper is biodegradable doesn't mean it biodegrades. In order to disintegrate back into the soil, it would need to be processed by microbes, fungi, and soil insects that break it down, eat and digest it, and excrete it. There's no way that's happening in a landfill. Sorry to burst the bubble. If you're putting them in your compost pile, that's another story. Just be sure to keep poop out of the bin.

Economics of Diapering

In the U.S., diapering a baby in disposables costs roughly $60 per month. Annually, that's $720. The average national age for U.S. potty training is 37 months.[7] So, non-ECing parents will usually spend about $2200 to diaper one child. It's helpful to know that the average EC'ed baby is potty independent at 18 months. So if you're crunching the numbers, you can budget about $1800 in diapers per EC'ed child. However, many EC moms claim that using disposables can increase a baby's potty graduation age.

For a basic stash of new cloth diapers, with about 36 prefolds and four to five covers, you'll typically spend about $300. Some parents choose more pricey options such as all-in-ones, or organic prefolds with wool diaper covers. Even then, it's rare to spend more than $1000—and your diapers will last through several babies!

Overheard...

We were given cloth diapers without a clue how to use them. We quickly assumed we must be doing something wrong, because the baby was constantly crying and wet. Didn't we just change her half an hour ago? Was this how often babies pee? In a few days, we figured out how to use the diapers, but had about 30 diapers to wash, dry and fold every day.

In a sheer moment of desperation, I figured there had to be a way to cut out the middleman—namely the diapers—so I held my daughter over the toilet and made the 'pssss' sound. To my complete amazement, she

*peed! I kept trying, and though it didn't always work, it vastly cut down
on the number of diapers we used. I'm grateful for every diaper we don't
have to wash.*

~*Nadine, mom to Geneviève and Elise Mirela*

You can scour the Internet to save on second-hand cloth diapers.
We'll address the yuck factor, because it's often the first question we're
asked. Cloth diapers can be cleaned easily and thoroughly. So, no, it's
not disgusting to buy used diapers, to reuse diapers, or to pass your
used diapers on to your next child. Each diaper should go through two
cycles—once in cold water to remove any soiling, and a second hot,
soapy wash to thoroughly clean and disinfect. If stains remain after
that point—sterile ones, mind you—you can bleach them by hanging
them out in direct sunlight.

Diaper-Free Time

Diaper-free time is simply that: a period of time during the day or
night when the baby isn't diapered. It can be a very helpful way to
launch your EC relationship and identify your baby's cues. Just take
off his diaper and observe. It's helpful to note what he does just before
and during pees and poops. These are his "cues." Once you've
identified a cue, you can offer the potty the next time you see it.

A naked baby can be incredibly daunting to a mom practicing EC
for the first time. Won't pee—or poop—go everywhere? Maybe. But
there are as many ways to enjoy diaper-free time as there are babies,
and you can do some experimenting to see what works best for you.

In warm weather, non-mobile babies can go diaper free on a
blanket outdoors. In cold weather, you may want to dress your little
one in some cute leg warmers, and put towels down on the floor. Some
moms don't mind a little sterile urine on the carpet, and quickly wipe
it up. Spray a 50/50 vinegar and water solution to zap stains and odor.

If your baby is mobile, it's a little harder to protect all surfaces.
Many moms find they have fewer misses when their baby is diaper-
free, as they're more tuned into cues.

It's important to note that most babies have a variety of signals,
depending upon the circumstances. While diaper-free time facilitates

Letting Go

By Melinda Rothstein, Co-Founder and Executive Director of DiaperFreeBaby

Many of us use "back-up" (i.e. diapers) to prevent accidents, messes, and often, embarrassment. But we need to be careful.

The longer we use "backup," the more we depend on it in ways we don't realize. And our babies do, too. Backup is just another barrier preventing us from giving ourselves over to intuition as a primary tool in tending to our babies' elimination needs.

In my experience, backup is good for a few reasons, which reflect our social norms:

-To protect our property, like rugs or furniture. [Materialism]

-To prevent having to change baby's clothes and parents' clothes. [Convenience]

-To avoid embarrassing situations. [Pride]

Of course, we have every right to use backup, and these reasons can be valid. But it's useful to consider when we use our reasons as excuses and when they are more urgent (i.e. you're bringing your baby to a wedding).

Forget about statistics, catches, and misses. Don't worry about the age at which your baby will take himself to the potty. That stuff doesn't matter. What matters most is that you trust yourself and your child. The rest will fall into place.

reading and anticipating your baby's cues, sometimes there are no perceptible cues at all. This can be frustrating, but stepping back and remembering that EC is relationship-oriented, not goal-oriented, helps.

Out and About

Some moms and babies enjoy heightened communication in a new environment: away-from-home pottying is a bull's eye every time. Other moms or babies get distracted, and pottying isn't center stage at the grocery store.

No matter which camp you fall into, once your baby begins using the potty consistently, it helps to ID the nearest bathrooms in your favorite haunts. Some babies do best on their own toilet—a petite potty with a discrete carrying bag can put a baby at ease pottying anywhere. If it's warm enough outside, there's no reason you can't squat in an out-of-the-way spot to offer a pottytunity!

Later Starters

The earlier you start pottying, the easier it is for a baby to catch on. Beginning EC after the baby is six months old may be more challenging. While it's still "premature" to the rest of our society, a baby has already begun to make the connection: diaper=toilet. Also, once your little one is mobile, new habits are harder to create. But don't let that deter you. The earlier you start, the sooner your baby regains awareness of his needs, and the easier toddler toileting will be.

The cornerstones of your practice are the same as any other ECer: help your child become aware of eliminations, observe his cues, and offer the potty. Diaper-free time is especially helpful to jump-start both his and your awareness of his eliminations. Switching from 'sposies to training pants or cloth diapers will help reinforce the new knowledge.

Overheard...

The biggest and hardest thing about EC in general, and late-start and part-time in particular, is to learn not to measure in catches.[2] If Elsie tells me what she's doing, signs, or learns her potty vocab, that's all progress. I'm happy for every morning my daughter runs around nakey-bum, and even for every puddle I have to wipe up, because we are learning. I am ELATED every time I catch a poop. I am tickled pink when Elsie tells me she has to go, or even that she's already gone in her diaper.

Most of all, I just feel like this is the way I want to do it. I don't want Elsie's potty learning to be some abrupt and sudden shift in her world. I want to introduce it young, and let her grow into it. It's fun to see the little steps along the way. If I waited for "readiness" I'd miss those daily joys.

~Kate, mom to Elsie

---

[2] ECers call eliminations in the potty "catches" and outside the potty "misses."

A Word to the Working: Part Time EC

Some parents choose to practice EC part time—for example, only in the mornings and / or evenings. Offering occasionally is fully in line with the practice of EC, and totally doable. Many Western moms don't practice 24/7 but still reap benefits. Offering the potty helps babies stay in touch with their elimination needs, regardless of how often the potty is offered.

Overheard...

When I'm with Henry, we do as much EC as we can, without stress. He goes diaper free for hours one day, and the next hardly at all. I try to catch his eliminations when he wears a diaper, but I don't worry about misses if I can't focus on it.

Cloth diapers are good for us since it is easier to tell how much he has peed in cloth than in disposables. When I know how much and how recently the baby has peed, I feel more confident about having diaper-free time without a mess.

~Maggie, mom to Henry

We EC part-time. We have days when we have a lot of misses, but it's no big deal. I often remind myself I'm not doing this primarily to save diapers. We recently started practicing EC while away from home, and it was easier than I thought. Family bathrooms are ideal for pottying on the go since no one looks at you funny if your baby pees in a sink!

~Francine, mom to Avi

Nighttime Pottying

EC's daytime benefits naturally extend to nighttime pottying as well. If your little one needs to go, and like many, doesn't want to soil himself, he'll find a way to let you know. Often mom thinks her baby is just a "bad sleeper" until she starts nighttime EC. Moms are often surprised to learn late night wake-ups often result from a full bladder, not a hungry baby. When the baby gets relief, he settles much more quickly, resulting in a better night's sleep for all.

For some babies, nighttime pottying is optional. A portion of these little ones don't care if they're wet at night. Others are dry all night long before they're dry during the day. But some babies prefer to potty at night. This is typically the case with those who are very sensitive to their pottying needs and prefer to stay dry.

Graduation

Moms practice EC to keep their babies dry and healthy, to build a close bond, and to spare the planet or their wallet. But we'd be lying if we didn't tell you we're also excited that EC babies are often out of diapers earlier, typically around 18 months old.

To keep the focus on communication and learning, the EC community refers to the independent pottying stage as "graduated" rather than toilet trained. But graduation means different things to different people. Some see it as the transition to undies, regardless of misses. Others reserve the title of graduate for children who can go to the toilet independently.

Regardless of when your baby gains independence, EC is a fun time of learning and communicating with your baby. If it becomes stressful, inhale, exhale, put your baby in a diaper, and take a break! EC is about the journey, not the destination.

Relate

connect from the heart

Can you believe your squishy little bundle will one day be standing on his own two feet, both literally and figuratively? It's enough to make us dab our eyes. We labor in love—teaching, guiding, stimulating, motivating, and socializing our sons and daughters. Mothers have enough hats to wear without being sold another by clever marketers, but unfortunately, that's exactly what happens. We filter products and make decisions that could affect our babies' long-term success, or so we're made to think. Your baby will be smarter if he has a light up drum that responds to his flailing arms. He'll be more athletic if you buy him a membership to baby gymnastics. He'll be more caring if you buy him a doll that says, "I love you." Of course, some of those things provide a few hours of fun, and aren't inherently bad. But do any of our "toys" really bring lasting joy? The phone, the handbag, the car? Maybe for a short time, but loving relationships are what truly give our lives color and significance.

Meaningful connection is the crux of this chapter. We want to help you push aside a thousand "shoulds" so you can focus on bonding with your baby without worrying if you're boosting his IQ. Once your baby gets that you're rock solid in his life, he'll be primed for exploring new territories and building new relationships.

Your role in the connection game? Forget the "educational" videos and bins of brain-stimulating toys. Instead, ramp up your focused attention (put down the smart phone…), get physical, and be willing to learn—from your baby. To cross some more items off your to-do list, we'll give you a few good (evidence-based) reasons why sharing, praising and even baby yoga can be overrated.

Attachment, Part Deux

In Touch we talked about attachment as it relates to physical touch. Now let's look through the lens of relationships with our babies.

Attachment can be used as a dirty word, especially in romantic relationships. We've heard some variation of, "She's so attached to him! He can't even go out with his friends." It's only slightly more acceptable in parenting circles, and even then, usually just for the first few weeks. But research is catching up with what most native peoples of the world have known instinctively. Attachment is actually a crucial foundation that sets up your baby for a lifetime of emotional health. Until we orchestrate a collective change of heart, though, it can feel like an act of rebellion to think outside the "infant independence" box.

Many moms breathe a sigh of relief to hear that their most important job during the first postpartum year is to create a strong bond with their newborn. Dishes can wait. Dust bunnies can wait, too. Even your hair won't complain if you go an extra day (or three!) without washing it.

Our tiny infants come into the world utterly helpless, and rely on us completely to get through each moment. A healthy attachment to mom fosters a baby's sense of security and wellbeing, which in turn builds emotional health, self-esteem, and lays the foundation for strong, loving relationships throughout life.[1]

In addition to birthing, holding, and feeding your baby with love, communicating—relating—is an essential tool to build a secure attachment with your baby. If attachment is so crucial, then why are we told to offer babies "brain-building" toys, rather than ourselves? Sadly, it's a cultural legacy handed down from opinion-based baby care experts who theorized (but didn't prove) that an intellectual approach primes babies for "success." While they may have us believe intellectual development is our primary job, emotional development is top on our babies' survival agenda. Heart first. All else will follow.

> *Many well-meaning moms and dads think their child's brain is interested in learning. ... It is a happy coincidence that our intellectual tools can do double duty in the classroom, conferring on us the ability to create spreadsheets and speak French. But that's not the brain's day job. ...We do not survive so that we can learn. We learn so that we can survive.*
> ~*John Medina*, Brain Rules for Baby

Attunement 101

One of the key ways to build your baby's confidence—and thus a healthy attachment—is through attunement, or being receptive when your baby tries to engage you.

Babies tend to engage their moms' attention in cycles. Just like the rest of us, babies like to be part of the action, but they also need some downtime to rest.

In a study on attunement,[2] researchers instructed moms to interact differently with their babies than they naturally would, in order to gauge babies' responses. When moms, as instructed, ignored their babies, the infants would flap about and look intently at their mothers, trying to get their attention. Getting no response from mom, the babies gave up, looked hopeless, and began self-soothing behaviors such as sucking on their fingers.

Why do we share this study, which wrenches our hearts each time we read it? To share a common-sense message about parenting and connection. As you know, attachment happens when a parent is in tune with her baby. Being in tune, from moment to moment, is as simple as observing your baby and doing what comes naturally in response. When her baby wants her attention, mom provides it, whenever possible. On the flip side, when he wants downtime, his mom gives him a break.

Providing a predictable and responsive environment is the first step in a lifetime of loving, effective communication. And loving communication is the foundation of a successful parent-child relationship. Don't worry: successful doesn't mean perfect. We're measuring success by a willingness to learn, roll up our sleeves and get dirty—playing with and working with our children. Here's the best part…it's so natural, we're willing to bet that you do it already.

The Parent Connection

Even the newest parents fall into default ways of interacting with babies. We pick up these habits in our childhoods, and later from society at large.

Babies are Born Innocent

by Jan Hunt, author of <u>The Natural Child</u>

What do you see when you look into the eyes of a newborn?

When I first looked into the eyes of my son, I saw trustfulness, curiosity and joyfulness. I saw no deviousness, meanness or selfishness. In that instant it became clear to me that if he ever acted in a devious, mean, or selfish way, his behavior would have been created by circumstances, not by him. In that instant, I knew what a great responsibility I had to honor and protect his innocence and joy in life.

Children are born innocent. They want only to be loved, to learn, and to contribute. Those parents who are not able to appreciate this truth miss what should be the most precious moment of their life. They cannot trust their child—they instead suspect him of being somehow flawed and requiring constant correction. The emphasis is on fixing something, not on enjoying and learning about this new person. The focus, from that point forward, is on the child's behavior, not on the parent-child connection.

A parent's attitude is absolutely critical in determining the kind of relationship they will have with their child. I find nothing sadder than meeting a parent who has somehow missed seeing their child's basic sweetness and good intentions, and thus believes that punishment is necessary to set him on the right path. This parent is always watchful, looking for ways to correct the child, which stifles his natural exuberance. This kind of suspiciousness is self-fulfilling—the child who is punished responds emotionally—as does any other person—with anger and fantasies of revenge, and physiologically with a burst of the stress hormone cortisol. The parent then feels justified in continuing and even escalating the punishments. The child is then seen as potential trouble—as the enemy.

The parent who is fortunate enough to see in his newborn's eyes only love, curiosity, and joy, will continue to trust and enjoy her child.

Instead of looking for "misbehavior," this parent looks for ways to connect and to bring joy into their child's life.

This attitude is also self-fulfilling, because love begets love. The child responds to being loved and trusted as we all do—by loving and trusting in return.

What takes place at the moment a parent first looks into their child's eyes sets the stage for a lifetime of joyful connection or struggle. It sets the stage for a rewarding relationship of trust and connection, or a battle between adversaries. This first meeting carries the seeds of years of happiness or misery. For those who can see their newborn's innocence and pure intentions, parenting may be challenging at times, but never a burden.

Look closely at this new being. Learn from him how delightful and simple life is meant to be. It's just an instant of time, but once this truth is fully grasped, it lasts forever.

Before the fog clears, we may find ourselves jockeying for spots in preschool and telling our newborns what good poopers they are. We'll share the research on which popular parenting activities are more than just hype.

Sign Language

Infant signing is all the rage these days. But why should I schlep my kid to yet another class, you ask? Great question. Like anything else in this book, you're always free to opt out if it doesn't resonate with you.

We found signing invaluable because a baby's desire to communicate starts much earlier than his ability to speak. And we bet you're dying to know what goes on in that sweet little head of his. It can be very frustrating to babies—especially toward the end of their first year when they start having strong opinions about things—not to get their points across. So why not give them a hand?

Overheard...

Signing—even a few simple signs like "more," "milk," "all done," and "help"—dramatically increased my daughter's ability to communicate until she began to speak, and as a result, reduced her frustration levels since I had a clearer idea of what she wanted.

Signing is a no-brainer—all benefits, no drawbacks. My only caution is to set appropriate expectations on when your little one can sign back— some books made me think she'd begin signing at 7 or 8 months, when really I had to wait until about a year to see her sign.

~Jane, mom to Sarah

Research shows that learning sign language may boost a baby's cognition by 50 percent. Teaching infants to sign can improve attention focus, spatial abilities, memory and visual discrimination.[3] Want the DIY version? Read an infant signing book or watch a video on the topic (we've shared our faves at the end of the book). Or, host an informal sign class with moms who have begun signing. Many moms make up their own signs, too. Being consistent with the signs you choose is key.

"Good Job!"

It may seem a bit premature to talk about a cautious approach to praise during the first year of life. But, believe us, when you first see your baby pee in the potty or stack a few blocks, you'll want to sing his praises from the highest mountain. That type of spontaneous, joyful praise can be life-giving to mama and baby.

We're not advocating for a tight-lipped approach to parenting, but rather a less-is-more intentionality around praise. According to Alfie Kohn, author of *Unconditional Parenting,* praising trains a child to look outside himself for approval. We'll put it this way: when we tell our child "good sharing!" or even "good standing," we spark an instant high in them, similar to our experience when buying really cute shoes, or eating chocolate. While both parties feel good in the short term, your baby will continue doing things to replicate that high. The danger in this habit is twofold.

First, our positive attention is conditional. It's being given in response to an action that we judge as favorable. And in the act of rewarding him or scolding him based on our subjective judgments, we're teaching our baby to adapt his expression to suit others' tastes. Bestowing lifelong moral values to babies isn't what we're questioning, but rather controlling behaviors for our short-term convenience. Like, you're really annoyed when your little one discovers his voice and screams as loud as he can to test it out, or decides that toilet independence means having the freedom to poop on the rug. Again. Raising a truly independent, confident child means allowing him freedom of expression, no matter how inconvenient it may be.

Second, external praise is on our hit list because babies don't internalize the lessons we intend to teach. They are merely repeating an action in order to get the reward we have given in the past. Rather than engaging in this short-term behavior modification, Kohn suggests we help our children understand our perspectives and form their own conclusions through discussion, observation, and asking questions. The result is a child who has truly bought in to his activities, and therefore acts from intrinsic motivation. A kid who wants to help prep dinner because he values home-cooked meals? We'll take it!

Of course it's not always so black and white. This is a *theory*, and since every child and every family is different, it's your job to put into practice what works best for your family. If you want to give it a shot, you're probably wondering what you'll do when your baby has a rock star moment, which happens, like, every five minutes.

Some tools that worked for us include making observations or asking questions. Telling a baby "you ate a whole carrot today" isn't a judgment of value, it's a statement of fact. It provides the language that your baby will connect with his activities, and it lets him know you're paying attention. Alternatively, asking questions like "did you enjoy that carrot?" tells him you're interested in his opinion, and sets the stage for reciprocal conversations in the future.

Ditching Mr. Fix-It

After the early months of soothing cries and wiping tears, it's hard to shift gears when our budding toddlers begin to learn about disappointment. And yet, there's great freedom in the acts of being an "agent of futility" and "angel of comfort," terms coined by Gordon Neufeld, author of *Hold On To Your Kids*. Neufeld suggests parents hold back their desire to fix things. In real life, this means explaining reality to your baby, as in "there's no more." Instead of diverting his attention, consider letting him work through it...even if there are tears.

Distracting a baby from loss is an emotionally charged act. We don't want our baby to cry, so we hand him a toy to redirect him. Lawrence Cohen dubs this a "quashing" of emotion, one of our

Miriam's Coaching Corner

Emotion

Even if you're on board with welcoming your child's full arc of expression, it's not always as easy as it seems. Thanks to our own experiences, we often panic or even feel angry when our babies are challenged. These reactions are perfectly natural. Try changing our mindset about the value of "negative" experiences happens over time, and we're sure to hit a few walls on the way.

Here's a scenario to help prepare you for the challenging emotions that arise when you experience the world as a parent. You're at a party, when your ten-month-old points at a toy car held by a two-year-old. The toddler yells "No!" and hits your angel on the head with the car. You're concerned for your baby, and fuming with anger. What to do?

1. Deal with the situation at hand. What does your baby need? How can you support his need to express his emotions, and create distance from the other child? Your baby can move on much more quickly than most adults. After all, he has no emotional baggage to carry. Once he's safe, tend to yourself.
2. Name your emotions. You can speak out loud for the sake of your baby, or in your head. "I'm angry." So often we try to brush it off, to avoid acknowledging how we feel. It doesn't actually work. And guess what? You have every right to be pissed off.

3. Relax your body. Close your eyes; just sit with the emotion. Notice where you feel it in your body and what sensations arise.

4. Be compassionate. When we resist emotions, they build up in our system. Children release old emotions through tantrums or crying, but we don't always have those luxuries. Summon the compassion you'd offer if a friend were crying on your shoulder. It's surprising how healing this can be.

society's drugs of choice. The challenge is, that emotion—whether it's frustration, anger or sadness—will need to find a way out at some point. So it's either now or in Aisle 7 of the supermarket. Instead of trying to keep the peace and placate your baby, Cohen suggests allowing him to feel the loss of a plaything.

When we distract a baby from his emotions, we're teaching him that reality is too harsh for him to accept, and that he should find solace elsewhere. Sound familiar? Yup, shopping, eating, drinking and smoking are all activities that adults use as distractions when life gets too hot to handle. Where do you think we learn this behavior? Hint: it all starts with "Don't worry about that—look at this!"

When you get down to it, there's almost nothing your baby can't handle with a loving caretaker by his side. When the going gets tough, let him know it's okay that he's sad/mad/frustrated, and that you're there for him while he sorts through his emotions.

A Bottle of Tears

Allowing your child to cry in the presence of a caring adult is a very different approach than "crying it out." Letting your child fully feel his emotions while you comfort him is healing. When reality conflicts with our expectations, it's disappointing. Not allowing ourselves to process those hurts—big or small—sparks unnecessary fear and builds a bottleneck of pent-up emotion. Allowing your baby to experience a range of emotions sets him up for emotional competence in the future.

The Joneses

We've entered into an age of hyper-parenting. With achievement, independence, and happiness at the top of most parents' wish lists, we often feel pressured to give Junior the best opportunities to develop intellectually, physically, socially, etc. We live in a world of resources, and, beginning as early as a pregnancy test, it's easy to go overboard and over-schedule ourselves and our babies.

According to Dr. John Medina, developmental molecular biologist and author of *Brain Rules for Baby*, hyper-parenting can actually cause the opposite of the "success" we desire to see in our children. For example, a child who is encouraged to learn basic math skills before he's ready may memorize the answers in order to please his parents. This is actually lower-level thinking that later needs to be unlearned.

In our era of growth charts and developmental delays, it's easy to get paranoid about your baby's trajectory. If you find yourself looking at baby Jones and wondering how you might prompt Junior to crawl, walk, talk, or even drool, keep in mind that no two children develop at the same rate. Further, just because baby Jones rolls balls to mom at seven months doesn't mean there's an NBA contract in his future.

It's just a snapshot in a long timeline of development and not a predictor of success. The pressure we put on our kids can actually extinguish their curiosity and may lead to toxic stress. As ice-cream makers Ben and Jerry say, "If it's not fun, why do it?"

Overheard...

I've felt the pressure to enroll in (expensive!) classes from other full-time mom friends, but recently committed to not giving in. There are so many affordable resources, and my son and I enjoy time to just relax and play together.

~Sarah, mom to William

The Budding Socialite

We're social creatures. When our babies smile at us for the first time, it lights us up inside, driving home the truth that we're better together. While there's no special formula for learning how to relate to others, a healthy dose of play each day will give your baby plenty of practice.

Interactive Play

Parents today are often insecure about exactly how to play with their babies, partly thanks to aggressive toy marketing campaigns that promise to boost IQ and make yours the smartest baby on the block. How can a regular parent compete with that? We're given the message that parents are simply not good enough, and that we'd better start shelling out the dough to educate our kids—immediately—if we want them to succeed in life.

We have really good news for you.

Love in the form of cuddles, affection, and rough and tumble play is the best gift you can give to your little one. There's even science behind this deceptively simple theory.[4] Think flashcards are where it's at? Not quite. The brain is all about interconnections. Flashcards are a one-dimensional experience. But cuddles and play activate multiple parts of the brain at same time, triggering the greatest growth.

According to child psychologist and *Playful Parenting* author Lawrence Cohen, active play is a feast for all the senses, firing away rapid connections in the brain. Physical interaction includes a healthy mix of auditory tones as you giggle, shriek, pretend to cry or "eat" your little one. It also introduces different skin sensations, from rolling on a rug, to jumping into couch cushions, to the touch of your skin or hair. Your baby's sight is stimulated by funny facial expressions and movement. Not only is goofy play great stress relief, it's the best brain builder around.

Open-Ended Play

Ever wonder why babies are so interested in boxes, bags, and tissue paper? These "raw materials" have infinite uses. When we bring home a thingamajig that sings, rubs its belly and turns tricks, its purpose has already been designed. For a baby who is beginning to explore his world, the throwaway items we take for granted are the building blocks of their world. How would you know that a paper bag could be used to store things until you've stuck your arm inside? Or that dirt and water make mud, unless you've had the freedom to mix them together? While marketers will pitch you on that singing thingamajig, consider saving your money and handing the baby a shoebox instead.

But open-ended play isn't all fun and games. Kids given free time to explore and play learn to engage with the world, practice decision-making skills, and resolve conflicts. Play also fosters healthy brain development, and equals less stress for the player.[5]

Toys, Schmoys

If the best kind of play is loving, physical interaction, then a baby's best toy is his parent! We don't need batteries, and we don't cost money. But Mom and Dad sometimes run out of songs and games. Toys can be great for introducing a variety of tactile and sensory stuff. They offer the gift of novelty.

Overheard...

I got addicted to buying toys. They were all over our home. One day, my husband asked me what Emily would do if she only had a ball to play with. I realized her imagination would soar. She might sit on the ball, roll it, or bounce it. She might pretend it's a balloon, or a bird. She wasn't deeply playing with any toy because she had hundreds. She was just skimming the surface of play.

So, I packed up most of her toys. Right away, I could breathe deeper. I can only imagine how it impacted my 2 year old! Now she plays deeper and longer with fewer toys.

~Alicia, mom to Emily and Oliver

What Makes a Great Toy

As you know, there's a lot of crap out there. Cohen uses this rule of thumb for purchasing toys, "The toy has to be more interesting than the box it came in." While navigating the world of playthings can be daunting, consider these simple areas before you buy:

Use. Does this toy allow for open-ended play? Will it foster creativity and imagination? Generally toys that replicate existing commercial characters don't leave much room for new discoveries and uses.

Durability. Will it last through multiple children? Is it made from sustainable materials? Is it easy to clean?

Longevity. Can this be used and enjoyed through multiple stages of a child's development?

While it's fun to see a baby's face light up as brightly as a new battery-powered toy, check your house for props that he might enjoy. Spoons, bowls, baskets with cloth napkins, and tightly sealed jars filled with wine corks fascinate babies.

Sharing

It's nice to share, right? I get some, you get some; we're all happy. Isn't that how it works? Well, not really. We like to think life is about everyone getting a little piece of the pie, but as most people can attest, whether emotionally, physically, or otherwise, sharing isn't always in the cards.

Still, at playgroups and on playgrounds, even with babies under a year old, you'll hear mothers exhorting their children to share, or rationing toys like meat during the Great Depression. Sometimes our motives are altruistic—Sally really deserves a turn with that truck. Other times our feathers are ruffled when another child swipes a toy from Junior. To further complicate the issue, our pride is at stake: a baby who shares is considered good. No one wants to be the mom of the grabby kid.

So what's a mom to do? Forcing your baby to share when he's this small is futile. Trust us. And, it might not even be in his best interest. Cohen gave us some of his sagest advice for babies' first year.

Trying to get babies to share is an exercise in vanity, because there are tasks they need to experience first. Like, reality. Loss happens. Babies just don't understand that, and their first year is too early for moral reasoning. Teaching infants compassion, and asking them to consider others by sharing is just not developmentally appropriate. What a baby most needs is a safe zone to experience his emotions.

Instead of rationalizing when your baby loses a toy, or scolding when he snatches one, try mirroring what you see going on with him. "Are you upset because Jaden took your truck?" Tone of voice and facial expression are powerful signs you get what he's going through. A baby may not understand your words, but he does sense your empathy. Use a soft, sad tone to explain that you know he wanted that truck, and it's okay to cry.

Television: Broken Connection

Yup, we're going there. You've probably heard by now that babies are better off without TV—or any screen time at all—before age two. And yet you've also heard of all those fabulous educational videos that can teach your child a second or third language before he turns two.

Here are some scary stats: for each daily hour of TV a little one watches under age three, his likelihood of having an attention deficit by age seven increases by 10 percent.[6] Even when the TV is left on in the background, it diverts a baby from his job—connecting with and learning from you.

Yes, it's rough to cut out TV, especially when all you want to do at the end of a long day is relax. But television is actually a stimulant. So watching TV before bed doesn't help us sleep, it actually wakes us up. And we all know how precious sleep is during a baby's first year.

Connecting the Dots

Everyone and their grandmother will tell you what's best for your baby. Then they'll tell you how much it costs, and whether you can pick it up at your local toy store or ship it direct from Amazon. But the most important thing you can give your baby—the most nurturing, the most educational, and the one he'll never grow tired of—is your love. This love manifests through your arms, words and songs, play, and most of all, your loving presence.

So please, don't let anyone tell you that your baby can have it all for just $15.99. You can already give your munchkin the world—for free. And by giving your baby your complete attention, be it once a day or as often as you think of it, you also give yourself the benefits of living in the moment, of seeing the world with the wonder of your baby's new eyes. So, dust off that goofy grin, throw your parenting books aside (yes, even this one), and do your best rendition of "She'll Be Comin' Around the Mountain" while you tumble with your little one on the floor. If you remember nothing else about this chapter (or this book, for that matter), know this: you are the most important gift that you can give to your child.

Eat
enjoy food together

Yes, we've heard the hype about baby cereal and baby food. Sounds delish. But we've bucked the system and had a fabulous time of it. We're excited to share one of the best-kept secrets in Nuevo cuisine: baby-led solids.

Baby-led solids are exactly what you'd think. We offer food to babies, and let them choose how, what and how much to eat. Rather than pureeing and spoon-feeding, food is cut so that a baby can grasp, suck, and gnaw: much less work for us, and way more fun for the baby. But the baby food industry won't love this budget-friendly, baby-centered way to introduce solid foods.

Wondering about choking, food allergies, messes, and babies who choose not to eat? We did too. You'll find your answers in the upcoming pages, and you may just have yourself a Homer Simpson moment: Doh! Why not make mealtime fun and easy?

Overheard...

I realized we were on to something when talking with a mom of an eight-month old. She said he'd gag when a Cheerio touched his lips, he was so afraid of texture! She just couldn't get him to eat.

I started to notice how often moms complained about mealtime—how stressful it was or how their child refused even the tiniest lumps in their food. I began to appreciate how eager an eater my little girl was! I'd never describe our mealtime as stressful—it's party hour!

~Bethany, mom to Sadie

The Science behind Baby Food

Who knew a blender could be so profitable? Baby food is a thriving $1.25 billion industry in the U.S. alone. The average American infant "consumes" 600 jars of baby food by his first birthday. We use the word loosely, as there's often as much puree *on* the baby as *in* the baby. Babies in Western Europe go through about 240 jars, and their Eastern European neighbors only taste an average of 12 jars in that first year!

According to Stanford University pediatrics professor David Bergman, "There's a bunch of mythology out there about [introducing solids]. There's not much evidence to support any particular way of doing things."[1]

Parents have been led to believe they're doing their baby best by offering pureed fruits and vegetables one. at. a. time. We interpret guidelines for food introduction as law, especially when coming from a pediatrician. Let's not forget that general pediatricians are not nutritionists, and their recommendations are often based on outdated and culturally-biased information. And that information was largely crafted and paid for by baby food manufacturers.

It's clear to many in the scientific community—and parents—that some of the standard early fare may not be best for a baby, after all. Rice cereal is among the top suspects. It's often given in bottle form and is many babies' first taste, aside from milk or formula. But, according to Dr. David Ludwig of Children's Hospital Boston, a specialist in pediatric nutrition, "These foods are in a certain sense no different from adding sugar to formula. They digest very rapidly in the body into sugar, raising blood sugar and insulin levels."[2]

There's a growing movement to get back to basics when introducing solid foods. It's been named **Baby-led Weaning** (BLW), by British pioneer, researcher and author Gill Rapley.

Keep in mind that in the UK, "weaning" typically refers to the introduction of solids, while Americans typically think of it as the end of breastfeeding. We'll call it baby-led solids to reduce confusion. Really though, it's been an unnamed way to feed babies for millennia.

Let's circle back to our purpose in writing this book: restoring the use of baby-care practices that are simple, natural, and intuitive. Give your baby what you're eating. Let him feed himself. Yes, it's that easy.

Why Let Baby Lead?

Self-feeding continuum. Breastfed babies have been self-feeders from the start, as it's impossible to force feed a nursing infant. These babies regulate how much milk they take in at each gulp, and each feeding. Encouraging independence with solid foods is a logical next step. If you have a bottle fed baby, letting your little one lead may be a bit harder (for you!) as you hand over the reigns, but your baby will love his freedom.

Exploration. The mantra "food is for fun" may help you wrap your brain around this principle. Babies learn by putting things into their mouths. Empowering them to experiment with foods allows babies a natural transition from milk to table food. According to Jessica Kosa, PhD and IBCLC,

> Most nutrition comes from milk for most of the first year for most babies. The half-and-half point in terms of energy intake is usually sometime during the second year. But there's a wide range of normal, and if you avoid empty calories, and offer nutritious foods in a pleasant social setting, it usually works itself out.

Daring divas. We've all met the child who lives on chicken nuggets and mac n' cheese. In fact, we may have been one of them. But studies show that exposing babies to a variety of foods from the beginning will expand their palate and may prevent a white-food-only diet from creeping in. A variety of flavors and textures also means he'll be more willing to try new foods when they're offered.[3]

Monkey see, monkey do. Babies love to imitate those around them. Whether they're clapping, smiling, waving, or putting a piece of fruit in their mouth, our little ones watch us very closely. It makes sense then, that mealtime is a perfect opportunity for social learning. If we park our baby in a high chair and feed him on his own for the first year or so, we're putting him at a disadvantage for developing social table manners. The baby who regularly eats meals with others learns about sharing, conversation, and the practical skills of eating.

Mighty mouths. All babies, whether or not they have teeth, develop the ability to chew. It's really just a developmental maturation and

Habits for a Happy Appetite

By Gill Rapley and Tracey Murkett, authors of <u>Baby-led Weaning</u>

Baby-led weaning (AKA baby-led solids) is a really obvious approach, once you know about it, but it was hidden until recently by two key things: the view that babies are incapable of doing much by themselves, and the belief that they need food well before six months.

When Gill worked with families with young children, she came across many parents who were experiencing problems with their babies' eating, especially from around seven months. She soon realized that if the babies were allowed to feed themselves, picky eating, food refusal and difficulties with lumps all seemed to vanish. It was the spoon-feeding that the babies seemed to be objecting to, not the food itself. When nutrition research finally came up with evidence that babies really didn't need anything other than milk until six months, the idea of avoiding spoon-feeding altogether was the logical next step.

By the time most babies' immune and digestive systems are ready to cope with solid food, they are also developmentally ready and able to feed themselves. Purees and spoon-feeding are only necessary for babies who are being given solids too early, or whose development is delayed. Babies of six months want to be independent—no wonder so many refuse to be fed!

Babies love being able to explore food at their own pace. With our current worries over fast food diets, eating disorders and obesity, it makes sense to have a healthy relationship with food from the start. Baby-led solids encourage relaxed and enjoyable mealtimes.
There's no pressure to eat a certain amount or a certain food and babies are able to utilize their natural appetite control to ensure they eat only as much as they need.

Baby-led solids respects babies' abilities, likes and dislikes, and nurtures skill development and confidence.

All of this resonates perfectly with parents who favor a more natural approach. As more and more families move away from parent-imposed regimes that go against their baby's instincts, baby-led solids are becoming an increasingly popular way to introduce solid foods.

Mealtimes are easier and less stressful for parents, with none of the food battles that are a feature of so many families. When children's choices are respected, and they are trusted to eat what they need from the beginning, mealtimes are more enjoyable for everyone. Continuing to trust children—and remembering not to hurry them or insist on clean plates—sets the scene for a lifelong good relationship with food.

coordination of muscles, like walking. Gill Rapley writes, "Learning to move food around your mouth is important for safety and good oral hygiene as well as for eating and speaking—and the best way to learn these skills is to practice them on lots of foods with different textures."

Overheard...

Think you need teeth to start eating solids? Not true! Anabella didn't get her first tooth until 17 months, almost a year after she started BLW! She and several of her toothless peers enjoyed gnawing on chicken legs, and biting off bits of apple with their healthy gums.

~Megan, mom to Anabella

Skills development. Parents of self-feeders often notice a speedy development of hand eye coordination. When babies begin shoving bananas and broccoli at their noses, it's hard to imagine they'll soon be able to use their pincer grasp to pop little lentils into their mouths. But it makes sense; babies who self-feed have more chances to practice hand-eye coordination. And while they chew, they strengthen facial muscles that they'll use to speak.

Overheard...

BLW was my saving grace! I wish I'd found it before we spent months trying to get Emily to eat purees—most of which she refused! The first time she grabbed a whole strawberry and devoured it, I felt such relief. I was nervous she'd choke, but the more I gave her, the more I saw that I could trust her. If a piece was too hard or too big, she'd just spit it out.

~Alicia, mom to Emily and Oliver

Why Wait for Solids?

The gut. It takes about six months for a baby's digestive system to mature. He sucks well, but doesn't have much saliva, which has enzymes that help us digest food.

Illnesses and allergies. Because the gut isn't fully sealed, allowing food particles to pass directly into the bloodstream, introducing solids too early can cause food allergies or other digestive illnesses, like Crohn's disease, colitis, or irritable bowel syndrome.[4]

The mouth. We use our jaw, tongue, and throat to chew and swallow food. Babies don't develop the ability to move food from the front to the back of their mouths to swallow it until they're around six months old. If you try to spoon-feed a baby before he's ready, you might notice he sticks his tongue out at you. He's not being fresh. Babies have a tongue thrust reflex that doesn't disappear until four to five months. It's nature's way of protecting his delicate system.

Communication. You know when your baby is tired or hungry in the early days (and later days!) because he cries. But if you're spoon-feeding him too early, he doesn't have the ability to turn his head and refuse food, which may result in overfeeding. And there's evidence that this could lead to confusion in his self-feeding regulation, causing problems with obesity in later life.[5]

Sleep much? It's a widespread myth that giving your baby solids will help him sleep through the night. Many babies begin to sleep longer stretches around three to four months, which coincides with the early start date for solids. The study "Infant sleep and bedtime cereal," in the *American Journal of Diseases of Children*, found no significant connection between feeding solids before bedtime and longer sleep.[6]

Weaning worries. Weaning, the process of gradually introducing foods and decreasing milk intake, can take as long (or as short) as you'd like. But if you start providing solids to a baby too early, your milk supply can decrease and lead to earlier weaning than you intended!

Megan, A Novel Mama

All Food is Baby Food

I love to eat. And cook. And eat. I spend most of my grocery dollars on food that's as close to its natural state as possible. I'm hooked on discovering new ways to prepare whole, real foods. The idea that I would feed my baby bland mush, or veggies that melted in her mouth like a potato chip, made me cringe.

I wasn't always this way. I distinctly remember telling my parents I didn't like asparagus or spinach when they were offered to me at about four years old. It took me twenty years to try—and like—either vegetable. Those weren't the only foods on my no-list. I ate my first orange in my sophomore year of college. Lobsters looked weird to me, so I wasted 25 years without crustaceans.

I didn't want Anabella to miss out on foods like I did, so BLW made perfect sense to me. Our families thought we were strange, and even careless at first. They didn't understand why Anabella was eating omelets at six months, or sharing our Seafood Newburg on Christmas Eve, or sucking on filet mignon at Sunday dinners. They were concerned about choking, and incredulous that she wasn't eating pureed sweet potatoes or cheerios or "normal" baby food. But after a few meals, she converted even the staunchest skeptic. For Anabella, all food is baby food.

Starting Solids: At a Glance

A few telltale signs can help you tell when it's safest to start offering your baby his first bites.

Sitting up unsupported. It's crucial that your baby is not reclining, slumping or falling over—those positions can pose choking hazards when eating.

Half birthday. Make sure your baby is at least six months old before he chows down.

Milk first! A hungry baby is a frustrated baby, and milk is fulfilling most of his nutritional needs in year one. Since he won't be ingesting much food in the beginning, a belly full of milk is the best warm-up for happy food exploration.

Obvious excitement. If your baby isn't interested in solids at six months, don't fret. Some babies are grabbing the food from mom's plate from an early age, while others prefer to wait as late as a year or more. Continue offering milk feeds and allow the baby to explore food when he wants. Try to keep things in perspective—one day you'll have trouble keeping up with his growing appetite!

In good company. Leaving a baby alone to eat is dangerous. Ideally, parents should be present when children eat for the first few years of their life. Choking is a concern in the early months of solids. In an optimal world, you and your baby break bread together, rather than you watching him munch.

What About Allergies?

With entire aisles of food that are nut-free, dairy-free, gluten-free, soy-free, and food-free, allergies are top on many new parents' minds. While we'd love a guaranteed way to avoid allergies, there's surprisingly little scientific evidence that pinpoints their causes, making it difficult to know how to keep your kids allergy-free.

Some societies are experiencing an explosion of modern-day food allergies. The number of kids with food allergies rose by 18% from 1997 to 2007.[7] In 2007, approximately 3 million U.S. children, about 4%, reported having a food-related allergy.[8]

Some scientists are backing a theory that our diet has a lot to do with the increase. A 2010 study compared the intestinal bacteria of children in Italy, with 14 children in a rural African village. The children in Africa who ate mostly locally grown fruits and vegetables had more diverse gut flora than kids in Italy who ate refined sugar, flour and high calorie foods.[9]

Another theory is that U.S. parents are introducing "high-allergen" foods too late. While some pediatricians advise parents to wait two or even three years before feeding shellfish or nuts, a 2008 study found that these delays may actually increase the risk of allergies.[10] The study looked at peanut allergies among children in London and Tel Aviv. British kids had significantly more peanut allergies, which researchers credit to the fact that 69% of the Israeli children received peanuts before nine months, compared with 10% in the UK.

Science shows that the best thing you can do to prevent your baby from developing allergies is to breastfeed exclusively through six months of age.[11] From birth until around four to six months, babies have a clean slate, intestinally speaking. Breast milk colonizes the infant's gut with disease-fighting, immune-boosting bacteria.[12] But it's not a surefire way to avoid allergies. Baby formula, unfortunately, is not on par with breast milk in the immunity department.

Sweet Temptations

If you're a pregnant mom with a serious chocolate craving, you may grumble at this section. But the research is undeniable. Sugar is chronically toxic. Yet consumption of beet, cane, refined, white, brown, and high fructose corn syrup continues to rise. We drink it, eat it, and crave it. And some people are betting we die from it.[13]

You won't have a heart attack after sipping a spiced pumpkin latte, but your body isn't happy. After years of binging on the sweet stuff, our organs get fed up. Sugar consumption plays a starring role in obesity, diabetes,[14] cancer,[15] heart disease,[16] digestive issues like Crohn's and colitis,[17] and hyperactivity.[18] But even if you escape some of the big guys, you're not running on premium fuel. Sugar provides a lot of empty calories, so we're filling up on nothing, rather than nutrient dense foods. To make things worse, refined sugar has absolutely no nutrients, forcing our bodies to kick it up a notch during digestion. Eating sugar depletes our internal supplies of vitamins, minerals and enzymes.

The old "moderation" line clearly isn't working. The average American consumes 22.2 teaspoons of sugar per day. The American Heart Association has a clear goal: women should consume no more than 100 calories a day of sugar (~6 teaspoons), and men's limit is 150.[19] Kiddos? Nothing. Zero. Zilch. They simply do not need and do not benefit from sugar, but tell that to baby food manufacturers—about 50% add sugar to foods for babies and toddlers!

The Scoop on Salt

Babies' developing kidneys can be badly taxed by salt. So it's best to stay away in the first few years. But you don't have to give up on flavor if you're sharing meals with a little one. Some parents use garlic, fresh or dried herbs, and spices. Remember: babies' palates are brand new. They don't know what they're missing, so they won't ask you to pass the salt.

No Choking Matter

Our first word on choking is that it's crucial to know how to handle it. We urge all new parents to take an infant CPR course, ideally before your baby is born.

Choking is usually the first or second concern parents have with a baby-led approach to solids. Keep in mind though, choking and gagging are different animals. Gagging is a safety mechanism that pushes too-big food out of a baby's airway. Gagging is usually—but not always—noisy, and can include coughing or sputtering, which works to help clear the airway. It can be scary to watch, but it lasts just a second or two. The occurrence of gagging tapers off altogether in a few weeks to a month.

Choking, on the other hand, is when a baby's entire airway is blocked. This means you won't hear anything. Choking prevents air or noise from coming out. If your baby is seated upright, and you allow him to put food into his mouth, rather than "helping" him, choking is no more likely than with a spoon.

In fact, your baby may be more likely to choke if you're spoon-feeding him, as it's easy to push food (especially stage two or lumpy food) down his throat before he's able to handle it. If he's developmentally able to get food to the back of his mouth unaided, then he's usually able to cope with swallowing it safely. So please resist helping put food in his mouth!

> **DISCLAIMER: NEOPHOBES**
>
> We told you that your child may become a gourmet chomper if you feed him from the table. While this often is true for babes who munch on their parents' meals, there's a very real phenomenon called "neophobia," which is the fear of new things...like food. It's a survival function that kicks in right around the time babies can walk, protecting them from wandering off and eating potentially dangerous foods. If we let our little one observe us eating the same thing, he knows it's safe and is happy to try it. Still, some kiddos rebuff all new food anyway. Though it peaks around two and a half years, don't worry, this phase eventually passes.

Another crucial tip: never put your finger into the back of your baby's mouth if you suspect that he's gagging. You risk lodging an item that your baby might otherwise easily expel. While you may have to sit on your hands at first, just watch your little one carefully to see if he's resolving the problem on his own—most often, he will.

The other major risk factor for choking is eating in a reclining position. It's important to wait until a baby's strong enough to sit on his own. Putting the baby in a secure and upright high chair (rather than a bouncy seat or reclined high chair) protects against choking.

Overheard...

There were no jars of baby food when I was born in Taiwan. Early on, my mom would chew up food, then feed it to me, so I ate what the rest of the family ate at their mealtime. Allergies were a non-issue. It was a very common practice back then, as saliva helps break down the food, making it easily digestible.

~Chialin, mom to Veronica and Antonia

FAQs on Baby-led Solids

What about drinks?

If you're nursing, continue to breastfeed as the baby requests. If your little one is thirsty, he'll nurse briefly—your smart cookie knows that the first sips of milk are quite thin. Since bottle-fed babies don't have the option of quenching their thirst with foremilk, offer a small cup of water with each meal. Juices and other drinks are unnecessary and are filled with sugars, spiking insulin levels and disrupting a baby's metabolism. It's best to stick with milk and sips of water.

How much should they eat?

Short answer: As much (or as little) as they want. Long answer: Remember, most of your baby's nutrition is coming from milk. In some cultures, babies are exclusively breastfed for a year or longer. By allowing your baby to explore, smoosh, throw, and occasionally eat his food, you're trusting that he knows best. A baby who's being fed milk has the luxury of playing with food as he starts eating, and will not starve himself.

Most healthy babies will feed themselves exactly what they need.[20] Resist the urge to jump in and help Junior on your quest for his acceptance into the clean plate club. Our interference can override his ability to know when he's full, leading to future weight problems.

It's hard, but please try not to compare. Different circumstances will lead babies to eat more at some times, and less at others. Teething, growth spurts, fatigue, a prior milk feed, and illnesses all play roles in the amount eaten.

If you're truly concerned that your baby is lethargic or failing to thrive, by all means call your pediatrician. But if your baby playfully mashes up his avocado and ends up wearing more than he consumes, take a picture!

How can I tell if he's hungry or not?

Signs your babe may want to keep going:
- looking intently at food on your (or his) plate
- manipulating it with his hands
- opening his mouth
- finishing all of a particular food

Signs your babe may be done:
- squirming in seat
- turning his head away from food
- throwing things on the floor
- spitting food out (unless he's gagging)

How many times per day should I feed him?
Some moms want a prescription for how many meals their baby should eat. At first, feel free to offer food whenever it works for you, maybe once per day, maybe more. Though there are families that start in with three meals right away, others gradually work up to that number. We've even heard a few moms quietly confess that they skip a meal or two here and there to avoid the mess or because they were tired. No guilt here: your baby won't suffer, since milk is his primary nutrition source!

What are some easy first foods to start with?
Anything relatively soft or juicy that can be presented in a French-fry-type shape, like:
- fruits such as apple or pear
- roasted veggies like sweet potato or cauliflower
- baked white fish or chicken cut into strips

What foods should we avoid?
First off, it's safest to steer clear of stuff that mom or dad is allergic to. We've found that lettuce or raw spinach can pose a choking hazard. In the earliest days, avoid round foods like grapes, nuts, and blueberries, as well. When we do feed these snacks, we like to cut them up the long way just to be safe.

In case you haven't already heard, consuming honey can put a baby at risk for botulism, particularly when raw. Babies are safe to try honey after their first birthday though.[21]

We both work; how can we start solids on our schedule?
If you're away from home for one or two meals a day, it may be daunting to adopt an unconventional approach to feeding. Given the right info, many day cares or nannies, can jump on board with baby-led solids. You may want to pack less messy foods for those meals, like cucumber slices or dried grass-fed beef sticks.

You can also mix it up and offer your baby purees part-time. If you think spoon-feeding will be easier for your baby's provider, you may want to have some soft food or purees ready to pop into the baby's lunch bag. But keep in mind—some babies who have been feeding themselves independently may resist being spoon-fed. There could be a power struggle brewing! Ask your caretaker to follow the baby's lead. If he wants to play with the spoon, let him. And make sure to pack enough milk to cover his needs.

Or, if you think you'd rather just stick with one method of feeding, remember—food is for fun! A baby doesn't need any nutrition other than mother's milk for the first year, so if you pack a bottle instead of food, your little one will be just fine.

Gear

Unlike nursing, feeding your baby solids will require a bit of gear. Most of it is your standard baby fare—high chair, sippy cup, bib (but since solids get super messy we recommend a smock), plates, and eventually spoon and fork. Sadly, most of the widely-available feeding paraphernalia is made from plastic. We get it. Not only is it cheap, it's easy to clean, and doesn't break easily. However, there are serious drawbacks to plastic: it's bad for babies, and it's bad for our planet. While tricky at first, we both managed to ditch 95% of plastic feeding gear for stainless steel, wood, even ceramic and glass. Straw and sippy cups tend to be the hardest spots to eliminate plastic.

Plastic, Plastic Everywhere

Plastic has become the go-to for many items, with special emphasis in the kitchen and playroom. The thought of ditching all your plastic may seem impossible. But it contains some hazardous materials. You've likely heard of "safer" plastics, and we'd like to give you the low-down on healthy plastics. But in good conscience, we can't.

Moms are smart. We get that the absence of data doesn't mean something is safe. We'll give you the low-down on why to avoid BPA, but that doesn't mean its substitutes are any less toxic. Manufacturers can—and do—replace BPA with untested compounds, and make a pretty profit before new health concerns hit the media. Instead of testing after products are on the market, which makes guinea pigs out of entire generations, we need policy change. Until then, we're doing our best to steer clear of plastic.

Environmental impact. Around 100 million tons of plastic are produced each year. Ten percent ends up in the sea, harming our fishy friends. The plastic that finds a home in our increasingly crowded landfills will see a millennium pass before it biodegrades. Many of us do the feel-good thing and toss our plastic containers in a green bin. But recycling used plastics often costs more than virgin plastic—economically and environmentally.

Bisphenol A (BPA). Consumer and environmental health advocates have brought BPA to light in recent years. Typically used in hard, clear plastics and in the lining of canned foods, BPA mimics estrogen and enters the body in its place. Even low levels of exposure can cause effects like obesity,[22] hyperactivity,[23] early onset puberty,[24] lowered sperm count,[25] recurrent miscarriages,[26] breast cancer,[27] and diabetes.[28]

BPA is found in water bottles and baby bottles, in linings of cans that contain food and beverages, including infant formula, in teethers and plastic toys. Many food prep items contain BPA: food processors, blenders, and water filters. Cans, receipts and dollar bills are the biggest source of exposure for pregnant women and babies. A 2010 study tested canned food bought at retail stores for contamination. Over 90% contained BPA![29]

Just because something is BPA free, doesn't mean it's safe, though. Studies have found BPA substitutes, like Bisphenol S and B, are endocrine disruptors as well.[30] And BPAF, BPA's fluoridated cousin, is even more potent than BPA.[31]

PVC. One of the most common—and concerning—forms of plastic is polyvinyl chloride, also called vinyl or PVC. An unstable plastic, PVC releases dioxin, a toxic chemical linked to health issues like cancer,[32] birth defects,[33] and damage to reproductive[34] and immune systems.[35] PVC is also softened using plasticizers called phthalates, which the Environmental Working Group has deemed unsafe for infants.[36]

Most plastic cling wraps and food storage bags contain PVC. All the money and care you've put into healthy food may be tainted by the storage method! Non-PVC wraps and bags are now available. Or consider green, reusable fabric snack bags. You can find them online or make them yourself.

Choose your Plates with Care

By Mia Davis, Environmental Activist

Plastic seems like the best place to store and serve our kids' food, for sure. It's cheap and practically indestructible. But it can be harmful, too. Food containers (and toys, and other household plastics) and the lining of tin cans often contain BPA or other hormone disruptors.

The brain is more vulnerable to chemical exposures during prenatal development and early childhood. Studies show that exposure to hormone-disrupting chemicals early in life may later manifest as fertility issues, behavioral issues, or cancers of the breast or reproductive organs.

Decades of research indicate that even very low dose exposures to toxic chemicals can have profound health effects. This counters the long-held tenant of toxicology that "the dose makes the poison"—the 16th century concept that basically says if ingredient X is deadly at 50 parts per million, for example, halving 50 parts per million and then halving it again will result in a safe dose, and anything lower than that amount is safe too.

Flawed thinking has shaped many countries' current chemical regulations and far too many companies' policies. There are several problems with the assumption that more of a given chemical is always worse for our health than less.

First, we now know that in some cases, low-dose exposures may have greater effects than higher doses. This is particularly true with hormone-disrupting chemicals, because very small amounts of hormone disruptors more accurately mimic the way our bodies produce and react to natural hormones (in tiny doses secreted by the endocrine system).

For example, if I dosed a lab rat with a ton of hormone-disrupting chemical, like BPA, the rat's cells would recognize it as a false signal. But if I dosed it with a tiny bit of BPA several times a day (the way we're exposed in life), its estrogen receptors would be fooled into thinking it was time to produce more estrogen. And more estrogen isn't a good thing.

Second, the "dose makes the poison" assumption overlooks the fact that many of the chemicals that appear in products are in other stuff that we use daily. Many small exposures actually add up to larger doses.

To add insult to injury, many companies don't tell us what they use in their products. Toy companies don't often tell us which plasticizers they use.

Producers of foam products, like breastfeeding wedges, do not tell us about the flame retardants they use. So parents can be at a loss, even when they're trying to read product boxes and labels.

And now for the good news: many of the health impacts linked to exposure to toxic chemicals may be prevented when we change the system that allows them on the market in the first place. When we tell companies that we want the safest products possible and will not buy products with toxic, untested or hidden ingredients, we make things better for all.

Non-stick pans. Teflon and other non-stick pans are cheap and simple to use. But they're coated with toxic chemicals. An Environmental Working Group (EWG) study[37] found that in less than five minutes, Teflon releases at least six gasses, two of which are carcinogens, and MFA, a chemical that can kill humans in low doses. Hundreds of pet bird deaths have been linked to the off-gassing of non-stick pans at high temperatures. The gasses caused birds' lungs to hemorrhage and fill with fluid.

Want safer options? Check out "Mother Nature's Finest" below. Or, if you'd like to use your non-stick pans, keep the stovetop at or below medium. And replace them once they're scraped; scratches expose unstable toxic compounds.

MOTHER NATURE'S FINEST

Looking to replace plastic in the kitchen?
Try these back-to-basics materials.

Glass is great to heat and store food, and even for cutting boards.

Stainless steel works well for water bottles and makes lightweight plates and cups for babies and toddlers.

Wood and bamboo make nice cutting boards but check your source. Bamboo is often bound with toxic glues.

Cast iron makes naturally nonstick pans and griddles that are easily cleaned and maintained.

Copper creates gourmet, healthy cookware.

Choose Your Own Adventure

There's no one-size-fits-all approach to feeding babies. We chose baby-led solids because it made the most sense for our families. We found that baby-led feeding met our shared value of having fun, and our hopes of raising children who have healthy relationships with food.

Now that you're armed with our favorite facts about feeding babies, the choice is in your hands. We know you'll find the solution that works best for your family. Eat, drink, and be merry.

Flow
letting go into joy

Before we bid you adieu, we'll tie together everything we've covered with some reflections on the new self who's emerging—the mother living the baby-led life. That's what we're really talking about here: responding to your little one's needs through the critical first year, when the foundation for health, relationship, and your baby's future worldview are laid. We know—it's not hip to put the baby first, but it's what nature intended. When we go with the flow, rather than against it, we're banking an investment of love that pays off handsomely— immediately and in the years to come. So sit back, grab a cup of tea, and learn how your mindset makes all the difference.

Overheard...

The best and most simple advice I've received is this: forget everything you've heard, everything you've read, and everything anyone has told you if it doesn't resonate with you. Take what you need and leave the rest. Your intuition and inner voice are the most powerful tools you have. Just make sure you keep an ear open because intuition usually speaks more softly than the rest of the noise.

~Alicia, mom to Emily and Oliver

The Unexpected

Expectations. We all have them. And, when we get real, we can see that they're the source of our trouble. If we go into parenthood thinking our lives will stay the same, our new reality can be shocking.

Most Western cultures' expectations of the baby experience go something like this: you have a pain-free birth thanks to an epidural or other intervention. You take your child home and put him in a crib soon after. He sleeps the whole night through, and begins taking regular, reliable naps. He cries a bit, but it's always clear why, and you're quickly able to learn why and to address his needs. You learn how to breastfeed without pain or trouble, or if you don't, it's easy enough to switch to formula, no harm done. Your baby fits into your schedule with minimal disruption. If he doesn't, you train him to. You continue your life as before, whether or not you go back to work, and your baby easily accommodates you.

When we expect our baby to accommodate us, we're in for a battle, because there's nothing in a baby's nature that has prepared him to ignore his needs. His survival instinct tells him to scream for all he's worth, and scream he will, until you respond or disconnect your ears from your heart.

But hear us and breathe: there's another way. If we shift our thinking from mourning and grasping for our old life to embracing our new one—focused on the needs of a dependent, helpless, pure little being—peace settles in. People often ask us, *"Don't you get burned out?"* Yes and no. Sure, we get tired like anyone else, but when you view this as a season, one you can never get back, there's a sweetness in it, a sacredness, a desire to cherish every moment. No one wants to look back on their child's first years and say, *we survived*. Instead, *we thrived*, is something we can all say—if we embrace our new reality.

Overheard...

When we decided to become parents, I had absolutely no idea what I was in for. All I knew was, it would be the hardest thing I ever did. I gave up any and all expectations of what my life was going to be like. And going into it like that was truly a gift. I didn't expect her to love me, nor did I expect myself to love motherhood. I expected hard work.

Once I got through the first three months, I realized I was in love—both with my baby and with motherhood itself. If I'd spent the year fighting for my old life back, I'd have missed the opportunity of a lifetime.

~Miriam, mom to Dalia

How to Flow Together

Letting the baby lead sounds nice. (Or maybe not, depending on your perspective.) But how does it work? First, throw out any and all expectations of yourself and your baby. Unsubscribe from those Babycenter.com emails if they're driving you crazy with unrealistic ideals. Here are some of the most common expectations that new moms tend to internalize: He should like the car. We should be able to get out of the house on time. He shouldn't cry in public (or really, at all). I should be able to manage the housework and take care of my baby. See a common theme? Yup, the word should. These "should statements" will drain the life right out of you.

Instead of yearning for what isn't, the best way to flow with motherhood is to recognize what is, and work within its parameters. More than that, find what you love about being a mama and focus on that. Your baby won't nap on his own? Make snuggling part of your daily ritual. He hates the car? Bundle him into a carrier and share an adventure on public transportation. He cries when you leave the house? Host playgroups in your home.

It's all in how you look at things. If you think a baby "should" fill-in-the-blank, which clearly he's not doing, you waste precious energy arguing with reality. And you can always find a friend or relative to back you up on that stance. The "shoulds" are where the disconnect happens and when we begin creating situations that don't respect a baby's unique needs. Crying-it-out, for example, was created as a "solution" to the statement "he should sleep through the night."

As Naomi Aldort, author of *Raising Our Children, Raising Ourselves*, likes to say, "the baby is always right." He cries when left to fall asleep at night? Something's not working for him—he's expressing a valid need. Contrary to popular opinion, babies do not manipulate. They aren't capable of it. So don't worry about getting hoodwinked by your little one. Instead, nurture your own soul by nurturing him. The thriving relationship you'll share, and the satisfaction of being in sync and being able to nurture your baby is unlike any job satisfaction we've known.

Overheard...

When considering self-care I think of the instructions at the beginning of a flight. Should an oxygen mask be released from above, you must put it on yourself before your child, though that fights a mother's instinct to care for your child first. I love my kids and they are one of the highest priorities in my life. But if they become THE top priority, I will fail them, mentally, spiritually, and physically. I'm not top priority either, but the foundation must be firm or the house will not stand. If I don't take care of myself, my children suffer.

~Katrina, mom to Nathaniel, Malachi, Joanna & Caleb

Handling the Haters

Valuing your self is only part of the equation. A human baby is born entirely dependent. If his mother, whose veins are coursing with nurturing hormones, doesn't look out for what she knows is her baby's best interest, it's unlikely anyone else will. Sometimes, especially during the vulnerable first year of being a new mom (and often long after) well-meaning grandmothers and aunts and friends and strangers offer advice on how your baby should be fill-in-the-blank (fed, diapered, held, etc).

If moms were incredibly confident with wills of steel, and took nothing personally, the effect of off-handed comments wouldn't be worth writing about. But the hair on the back of our neck rises when we hear: *"If you hold her too much, you'll spoil her." "Once she can ask for it, she's too old to be nursing." "Get her out of your bed soon or she'll be in there forever."* Unless you live in a cave, you're likely to hear some version of these words from family, friends and nosey strangers. It seems everyone over the age of eighteen is an expert in childrearing, and they all know your baby better than you do.

But don't despair. Sometimes it feels like no one understands, and that no one else has charted these murky waters, but that's simply not true. New moms are often baffled at how cavalier others are—especially moms of older kids—when it comes to parenting decisions.

Seasoned moms (and know-it-alls) can dole out advice with their eyes closed, and sometimes it comes across as law. Conversations about mothering can leave you feeling like you're doing something that will irreparably damage your baby, or that you're not as capable or competent as you should be. We'll give you the inside scoop though—nearly all the moms we talked to felt as though they bumbled through their first baby's year. And they confessed: it's easy to forget that vulnerable feeling.

Remember: the most important thing is that you feel comfortable with the decisions you make regarding your baby. You birthed your baby, and you are the best mother he has. Changing your game plan to satisfy others usually ends up frustrating mom, confusing baby, and generally doesn't last. So if you're struggling with the arrows of dissenters, stand your ground. You're in good company.

One of the best ways we've found to deal with "decision dissenters" is to be armed with information. Oftentimes people spout off clichés without giving them much thought. If you feel tongue-tied when someone questions you on a parenting practice that may not be mainstream, we encourage you to do a little prep work. You likely made certain decisions for specific reasons. Sometimes we forget exactly why we chose a certain path, though, other than it just felt right. Brainstorm some of the questions you get constantly, and devise a few stock answers. Often people are just uneducated about different ways of doing things, and may actually be grateful to hear your well-thought-out response.

Overheard...

We have some relatives and friends who, to put it gently, have "opinions" about how we should handle our baby, most of which relate to feeding and sleeping.

I breastfeed exclusively, and our son still has two overnight feedings. It seems like some people just cannot let this go and feel the need to constantly inform us that he should sleep longer, that he doesn't need to be fed overnight, that he's only feeding out of habit or comfort, and say really unhelpful things like, "He just has to learn to sleep on his own." Thankfully, my husband and I are 100% on the same page about what we do, and that helps tremendously.

~Heidi, mom to Sam

Taking the Struggle Out of Baby Care

By Naomi Aldort, Author of Raising Our Children, Raising Ourselves

By nature, lovingly caring for your baby is not a struggle, but an invigorating delight. Your baby makes no mistakes in needing whatever he needs; we are not here to fix nature's "errors" or to struggle against a "flawed" baby or child. Responding with our open heart may seem scary only because we have been trained not to trust ourselves. Yet your baby's cues are the perfect guide to achieve struggle-free parenting.

Mothers often describe times when they relinquish their own best sense about their baby in favor of impressing someone else or protecting another's feelings—sometimes even strangers in the park. However, you are not their mother; your baby counts on you to care for him first.

How did we lose trust in our own innate wisdom and love, and become so dependent on approval? Most of us were taught from the start to undermine our own wisdom and follow the direction of others instead. We were taught as babies and children to ignore our natural yearning to sleep with mom, to be held, and to be with our parents all day long. Sometimes we were left to cry our hearts out until we learned, "What I need must be wrong. I should not listen to myself. I should look for cues from others." This is how babies learn to be dependent and insecure, and later, become susceptible to peer pressure, media and outside influences.

Flowing with the baby is not neglect or passivity. It's the opposite. When we don't oppose the baby, we can lead the way with clarity, because we understand what he can and cannot handle. We don't pretend that he can handle shopping if he cannot, or that he is able to happily fall asleep without our presence. We act in line with reality, not with a fantasy fueled by the opinions of others.

"How will he ever learn to fit in if we don't teach him?"

Contrary to parents' fears, children don't need imposed lessons. They didn't need breathing instructions in utero either.

From my experience with hundreds of families worldwide, it is when babies are controlled, and their inclinations resisted, that they are likely to develop traits of anger, disregard for others and aggression, because they duplicate what they experience.

In contrast, a baby who feels nurtured will, over years, develop the same kind of care toward others. Babies who are raised with the utmost respect from infancy develop into children who behave well of their own free will, with no need for imposed discipline.

The baby whose needs are fully met learns true independence.

We often equate doing things by oneself with being independent. However, independence is the ability to rely on one's own inner guide, and it has nothing to do with being alone. For example, the baby's independent choice is often to sleep with his mother. When we reject his choice, we teach him to depend upon our direction. In contrast, when we honor the baby's need and sleep with him, he learns to trust himself: "My inner voice is right."

Parenting becomes exhausting when we struggle against the flow. If you find your baby difficult, take a breath and check if you're going against the stream. Change directions by finding a way to respond to and connect with your baby. Resisting the baby is difficult; flowing with the baby is easy and makes mothering the most invigorating, expanding and satisfying adventure you will ever experience.

Gal Pals, Mama Style.

Another way to nourish yourself is to find friends. Mom friends. You'll probably talk about nipple soreness and nap transitions and smelly poops, but that's okay. Your single friends don't want to hear it, and you could use an outlet. Even more importantly, it's crucial to normalize your day-to-day life. Sometimes we get so caught up in our own world, we forget that we're not the first, and won't be the last to be peed on, bitten, dog-tired, and worried about every little thing.

But more than being a normalizer, friends are a support system. They encourage you when you're down, hug you when you're sad, help you when you're tired, and offer advice that you may actually want to take.

So where are these future BFFs? Scout out your local library. Even small babies may enjoy a sing-a-long or story hour. Community centers often have free or low-cost classes for kids of all ages. If you're interested in EC, baby-wearing, or breastfeeding, check out your local chapters. Some larger towns have Yahoo, Big Tent or Meetup groups (Megan and Miriam met through an Attachment Parenting Meetup group!), where play dates are posted, issues are discussed and friendships are formed. Hanging out on the fringes of the group for a bit may help you figure out who's of like mind.

We're not saying ditch your old friends, or don't make friends with moms who are different, but we believe it is of the utmost importance that if you're going against mainstream culture, you find a way to tap into a network. Having friends who don't breastfeed or co-sleep may not seem like a big deal at first, but it may be more challenging to parent your way if you don't have a support system to troubleshoot and share joys with.

Overheard...

Motherhood is a rite of passage for women. To those who are already mothers, a new mom is joyously welcomed into the club. To those who are not moms, my shift in priorities isn't seen as an improvement. So musings about my child are reserved for members of that club who welcome me with open arms.

~Colette, mom to Millie and Sammy

Self-Love: Mama Edition

We're not asking you to become a shrinking violet, forego your career, showering, or your favorite hobby. Quite the contrary. In order to give to our babies, we have to want what's best for ourselves, too. Though it may differ from mom to mom, our basic needs tend to be a sense of physical health, emotional wellbeing, connections with like-minded families, and feelings of competence and confidence in our new role. But often one or more of these areas is put on the back burner when the baby comes.

You've heard it before (in modern society, we're willing to bet on it): make yourself a priority. This doesn't have to contradict letting the baby lead. While we're not advocating leaving your baby bawling.

Miriam's Coaching Corner

Synchronicity

Have you ever felt like you were in the zone? You were doing something you loved, or involved with something that captivated you—playing music, creating art or writing, for example. You just knew what to do, or even if you didn't, you were confident that what you needed to do would come to you. This is a state of being open to possibility, to intuition and inner guidance. When you're in the zone, there's a sense that all is well, and a heightened receptivity to ideas that can help you move further along the path.

Being "in the flow" is often reported by mothers who are attuned with their babies. Not only are we open to the most important clues—those babies communicate about how they need to be mothered—we're open to external ideas that can apply to our babies. This openness is what allowed me and Megan to find the practices that meant the most to us as mamas, like EC, baby-led solids, and co-sleeping. We didn't go into motherhood knowing that we'd parent exactly the way we do, but we picked up on cues in our environment that resonated with us as parents and with our sense of our daughters and their needs.

When you're attuned to the part of you that is wise, loving and open, you get the info you need, as you need it. When you welcome your mama instinct, your love of nurturing that makes each day shine, you'll receive all the tools you'll need to parent your child.

while you go on a spa day, you can find a happy medium. Recognize your top needs and find ways to feed them, even if it's just a little bit here and there. Is a shower what you need to feel human? Find a way to bring the baby in, hand him off to dad, or shower while he sleeps. Does yoga help you find your center? Check out a baby and me class, or do downward dog over your little one as he lies on the floor. You're more interesting than his mobile, anyway!

Western societies tell mothers we can do everything, and by doing so often imply that we should put ourselves last. We're advocating for a strategic straddling of the two. You can't do everything, but you can nurture yourself in the way you need most, if you're creative about it. Make sure you know what really fills your tank these days—not what you used to need, or what your single girlfriends say you need—and make it happen.

Rock on, Mama!

If you forget everything else you read in this book, there's just one message we want you to take away. You are the mother. The fact that this greatest of honors has been bestowed on you is significant. It means you're fully loaded: you've got all the internal resources you need to raise your child in the way he most needs. You have the intuition, the knowledge and yes, the courage, to reach inside yourself and find the answers that will help him thrive.

Babyhood is a time of unfolding, and it's our privilege to witness and embrace this crucial year. We're so very excited for you as you embark on the magical journey of motherhood. You're on the ride of your life. So take a deep breath, and hold on tight.

Parenting will turn you upside down and inside out, shaking the very foundation of the world as you knew it. It's a total revolution. And the best way to rock a revolution is to become a revolutionary.

Authors' Helpline

Find Yourself in Mothering

Miriam J. Katz is a Certified Professional Coach who supports conscious new parents in all aspects of their journeys. Through skilled facilitation, Miriam can help you find your own authentic answers to the big questions, such as *Who am I?* and *What are my core values?* The answers to these questions lay a solid foundation upon which to choose your parenting tools and lay plans. Contact Miriam for a free initial consultation at Miriam@theotherbabybook.com or visit www.miriamjkatz.com.

Mama: Nurtured

Megan McGrory Massaro spent nearly a decade as a youth educator. Today, she educates new mothers, grandparents, and caregivers with her expertise in natural, traditional parenting practices. Megan specializes in creating action plans for busy parents. Looking to set up a sleep arrangement that works for everyone, go diaper free, or plan your foray into baby-led solids? Need some practical nursing advice or strategies to improve your weekly meal preparation for your family? Contact Megan for an individual consultation at Megan@theotherbabybook.com.

Acknowledgments

Our deepest thanks to Anabella and Dalia, our muses, and Mark and Misha, our partners, who made this book possible.

Special thanks to our panel of moms and chapter experts (see **Intro**), and our editors: Mona and David Abramson, Naomi Aldort, Beth Bejnarowicz, Karina Dyer, Jean Jewell, Chialin Kao, Ted McGrory, Mollie McGrory, Lani Michelle, Francine VanWoudenberg Sikkema, and Melinda Rothstein. Our deep gratitude to Barbara Nicholson and Lysa Parker for their heartfelt introduction to our work.

We're grateful to *The Other Baby Book* team, who supported us immensely with their time and love: Alicia Clare, Adrienne Gager, Amy Keighley, Rachel Morgan, Bethany Sheets, Candy Yau and our fabulous Facebook volunteers. Kudos to Sarah Georgakopoulos, the most amazing cover designer we know, inside and out. We'd also like to thank Winifred Golden for believing in us.

Join Our Community

Web: www.theotherbabybook.com

Twitter: @OtherBabyBook

Facebook: www.facebook.com/TheOtherBabyBook

The *Other* Baby Bookshelf

Birth

Spiritual Midwifery and *Ina May's Guide to Childbirth* by Ina May Gaskin

The Business of Being Born and *More Business of Being Born* (DVDs) by Ricki Lake and Abby Epstein.

Natural Health After Birth and *Vaccinations* by Aviva Jill Romm

Smart Medicine for a Healthier Child by Janet Zand, ND

Natural Baby and Childcare by Lauren Feder

Touch

Touching by Ashley Montagu

Babywearing by Maria Blois

The Vital Touch by Sharon Heller

Babywearing International (babywearinginternational.org)

The Babywearer (thebabywearer.com)

Skin Deep Database (www.ewg.org/skindeep)

Milk

Breastfeeding Made Simple by Nancy Mohrbacher

The Womanly Art of Breastfeeding by La Leche League

Nursing Mother's Companion by Kathleen Huggins

Nursing Mother, Working Mother by Gayle Pryor

KellyMom (KellyMom.com)

Mother-to-Mother Nursing Support Groups
- Breastfeeding USA: www.breastfeedingusa.org
- La Leche League International: www.llli.org
- Nursing Mother's Council: www.nursingmothers.org

Sleep

Three in a Bed by Deborah Jackson

Sleeping with Your Baby by James J. McKenna

The No-Cry Sleep Solution by Elizabeth Pantley

Notre Dame Mother-Baby Sleep Laboratory www.cosleeping.nd.edu.

Potty

Diaper Free! by Ingrid Bauer

Infant Potty Training by Laurie Boucke

The Diaper-Free Baby by Christine Gross-Loh

Nappy Free DVD by Nicole Moore

Relate

Playful Parenting by Lawrence J. Cohen, PhD

Unconditional Parenting by Alfie Kohn

Sign with Your Baby by Dr. Joseph Garcia

Brain Rules for Baby by Dr. John Medina

Attached at the Heart by Barbara Nicholson and Lysa Parker

Eat

The Baby-led Weaning Cookbook by Gill Rapley and Tracey Murkett

Real Food for Mother and Baby by Nina Plank

Nourishing Traditions by Sally Fallon and Dr. Mary Enig

Flow

Raising Our Children, Raising Ourselves by Naomi Aldort

Parenting for Peace by Marcy Axness, PhD

The Continuum Concept by Jean Liedloff

The Natural Child Project (naturalchild.org)

Attachment Parenting International (attachmentparenting.org)

Mothering (Mothering.com

Chapter Notes

Birth

1 Sutton, J, P Scott. *Understanding and Teaching Optimal Foetal Positioning.* New Zealand: Birth Concepts: 1995.

2 Declercq, E, C Sakala, M Corry, and S Applebaum. "Listening to Mothers II: Report of the Second National U.S. Survey of Women's Childbearing Experiences." MS; January–February 2006 for Childbirth Connection by Harris Interactive® in partnership with Lamaze International.

3 Ehrenthal, D, X Jiang, D Strobino. "Labor Induction and the Risk of a Cesarean Delivery Among Nulliparous Women at Term." *Obstetrics and Gynecology* 116.1 (2010): 35-42.

4 *Oleson, O. Meta-analysis of the Safety of Home Birth. Birth 24.1(1997):4-13.*

5 MacDorman, M. F., Declercq, E. and Mathews, T. J. (2012), Home births in the United States, 1990–2009. NCHS data brief no. 84. US Department of Health and Human Services, CDC, National Center for Health Statistics.

6 Frye, A. Holistic midwifery: A comprehensive textbook for midwives in homebirth practice, volume I, care during pregnancy. Portland, Oregon: Labrys Press, 1995.

7 Butler, J, B Abrams, J Parker, J Roberts, R Laros. "Supportive nurse-midwife care is associated with a reduced incidence of cesarean section." *Am J Obstet Gynecol* 168 (1993): 1407-13.

8 Greulich, B, L Paine, C McClain, M Barger, N Edwards, R Paul. "Twelve years and more than 30,000 nurse-midwife-attended births: the Los Angeles County + University of Southern California women's hospital birth center experience." *Journal of Nurse-Midwifery* 39.4 (1994): 185-96.

9 "Direct-Entry Midwifery State-by-State Legal Status." Chart. *Midwives Alliance of North America.* MANA, 11 May 2011. Web. 12 July 2011. <www.mana.org>.

10 Creedy, D, I Shochet, J Horsfall. "Childbirth and the Development of Acute Trauma Symptoms: Incidence and Contributing Factors." *Birth,* 27 (2000): 104–111.

11 MacDorman, MF, E Declercq, and J Zhang. "Obstetrical Intervention and the Singleton Preterm Birth Rate in the United States from 1991-2006." *American Journal of Public Health* 100.11 (2010): 2241-247. Print.

12 *The Business of Being Born.* Dir. Ricki Lake and Abby Epstein. Rede Entertainment, 2008. DVD.

13 *Giving Birth.* Dir. Suzanne Arms. Suzanne Arms Presents, 1999. DVD.

14 Alexander, G, C Korenbrot. "The Role of Prenatal Care in Preventing Low Birth Weight." *The Future of Children* 5.1 (1995): 103-120.

15 Kruckman, L. "Rituals and Support: An Anthropological View of Postpartum Depression." *Postpartum Psychiatric Illness.* Philadelphia: University of Pennsylvania, 1992. 137-48. Print.
Stern, G, L Kruckman. "Multi-disciplinary perspectives on post-partum depression: An anthropological critique." *Social Science and Medicine* 17.15 (1983): 1027-1041.

Locicero, A, D Weiss, D Issokson. "Postpartum depression: Proposal for prevention through an integrated care and support network." *Applied and Preventive Psychology* 6 (1997): 169-78.

16 Deshpande, A, J Gazmararian. "Breast-feeding education and support: Association with the decision to breast-feed." *Effective Clinical Practice* 3.3 (2000): 116-22.

Morrow, A, M Muerrero, J Shults, J Calva, C Lutter, J Bravo, et al. "Efficacy of homebased peer counseling to promote exclusive breastfeeding: A randomised controlled trial." *Lancet* 353 (1997): 1226-31.

Giugliani, E, J Vogelhut, F Witter, J Perman. "Effect of breastfeeding support from different sources on mothers' decisions to breastfeed." *Journal of Human Lactation* 10.3 (1994): 151-161.

17 Porteous, R, K Kaufman. "The effect of individualized professional support on duration of breastfeeding: a randomized controlled trial." *Journal of Human Lactation* 16.4 (2000): 303-8.

18 Swain, A, M O'Hara, K Starr, L Gorman. "A prospective study of sleep, mood, and cognitive function in postpartum and nonpostpartum women." *Obstetrics and Gynecology* 3.3 (1997): 381-6.

19 Ansgar, C, A Müller, S Doberenz, S Kim, A Meuret, E Wollburg, W Roth. "Psychophysiological Effects of Breathing Instructions for Stress Management." *Applied Psychophysiology and Biofeedback* 32.2 (2007):89-98

20 Goldberg, A. "Cervical Ripening." *Medscape Reference*. WEBMD LLC, 27 May 2011. Web. 17 Dec. 2011. <http://emedicine.medscape.com/article/263311-overview>.

21 Dublin S et al. "Maternal and neonatal outcomes after induction of labor without an identified indication." *Am J Obstet Gynecol* 183 (2000): 986-94.

22 Seyb ST et al. "Risk of cesarean delivery with elective induction of labor at term in nulliparous women." *Obstet Gynecol* 94.4 (1999): 600-7.

23 JHP Pharmaceuticals. *Pitocin Product Summary*. JHP Pharmaceuticals. *JHP Pharmaceuticals*. Web. 04 Jan. 2012. <http://www.jhppharma.com/products/pitocin.html>.

24 Kavanagh, J, AJ Kelly, J Thomas. "Sexual Intercourse for Cervical Ripening and Induction of Labour." 2 (2008). *Cochrane Systematic Database Review*. Web. 11 Dec. 2011.<http://http://summaries.cochrane.org/CD003093/sexual-intercourse-for-cervical-ripening-and-induction-of-labour>.

25 Controlled Therapeutics. *Cervidil Brand of Dinopropone Vaginal Insert*. East Kilbride, Scotland: Controlled Therapeutics, 2010. Print.

26 Podulka, J, E Stranges, and C Steiner. "Hospitalizations Related to Childbirth, 2008." *Healthcare Cost and Utilization Project (HCUP) Statistical Briefs* (2011). Web. 12 Nov. 2011. <http://www.ncbi.nlm.nih.gov/books/NBK52651/>.

27 Thacker SB, H Banta. "Benefits and risks of episiotomy: an interpretative review of the English language literature, 1860-1980." *Obstetrical & Gynecological Survey* 38.6 (1983): 322-38.

28 Osterman, M, J Martin. *Epidural and Spinal Anesthesia Use During Labor: 27-state Reporting Area, 2008*. Rep. 5th ed. Vol. 59. Atlanta: Center for Disease Control, 2011. Print.

29 iBid

30 Declerqc, E, C Sakala, M Corry, and S Applebaum. Rep. *Listening to Mothers II*. For Childbirth Connection by Harris Interactive, Oct. 2006. Web. 3 May 2011. <http://www.childbirthconnection.org/pdfs/LTMII_report.pdf>.

31 "Options: C-Section | Cesarean Section :: Childbirth Connection." Childbirth Connection: Helping Women and Families Make Decisions for Pregnancy, Childbirth, Labor Pain Relief, the Postpartum Period, and Other Maternity Care Issues. Childbirth Connection, 23 May 2011. Web. 04 Jan. 2012.

[32] Ehrenthal, D, X Jiang, D Strobino. "Labor Induction and the Risk of a Cesarean Delivery Among Nulliparous Women at Term." *Obstetrics and Gynecology* 116.1 (2010): 35-42.

[33] Hannah ME, Hannah WJ, Hewson SA, Hodnett ED, Saigal S, Willan AR. *Planned caesarean section versus planned vaginal birth for breech presentation at term: a randomised multicentre trial.* Oct 21, 2000. Lancet. 21;356(9239):1375-83.

[34] Declerqc, E, C Sakala, M Corry, and S Applebaum. Rep. *Listening to Mothers II.* For Childbirth Connection by Harris Interactive, Oct. 2006. Web. 3 May 2011. <http://www.childbirthconnection.org/pdfs/LTMII_report.pdf>.

[35] Guise, JM, et all. *Vaginal Birth After Cesarean: New Insights.* Rep. no. 10-E003. Regon Evidence-based Practice Center, Oregon Health & Science University, Mar. 2010. Web. 3 May 2011. <http://www.ncbi.nlm.nih.gov/books/NBK44571/>.

[36] Martin J, B Hamilton, P Sutton, S Ventura, et al. *Births: Final data for 2006. National vital statistics reports* 57.7. Hyattsville, MD: National Center for Health Statistics. 2009.

[37] Sakala, C. "Midwifery care and out-of-hospital birth settings: how do they reduce unnecessary cesarean section births?" *Soc Sci Med* 37.10 (1993): 1233–1250.

[38] Mercer J. "Current Best Evidence: A Review of the Literature on Umbilical Cord Clamping."*Journal of Midwifery and Women's Health*, invited, 46.6 (2001): 402-414.

[39] Gupta R, S Ramji. "Effect of delayed cord clamping on iron stores in infants born to anemic mothers: a randomized controlled trial." *Indian Pediatrics* 39 (2002): 130-135.

[40] iBid

[41] Higgins, A C Begley, M Nevin, et al. "A toolkit to support nursing and midwifery competency development."National Council for the Development of Nursing and Midwifery, Dublin (2010).

[42] Moore ER, G Anderson, N Bergman. "Early skin-to-skin contact for mothers and their healthy newborn infants." *Cochrane Database of Systematic Reviews* 3.CD003519 (1997).

[43] Newman, J. "The Importance of Skin-to-skin Contact." *Newman Breastfeeding Clinic & Institute.* International Breastfeeding Centre, 2009. Web. 08 Nov. 2011. <http://www.nbci.ca/index.php?option=com_content>.

[44] Barak, M, A Horn, N Bergman. "Should Neonates Sleep Alone?" *Biological Psychiatry* 70.9 (2011): 817.

[45] Moore ER, G Anderson, N Bergman. "Early skin-to-skin contact for mothers and their healthy newborn infants." *Cochrane Database of Systematic Reviews* 3.CD003519 (1997).

[46] Ludington-Hoe, S, S Golant. *Kangaroo Care: The Best You Can Do for Your Premature Infant.* New York: Bantam Books, 1993.

[47] Bergstrom A, R Byaruhanga, P Okong. "The impact of newborn bathing on the prevalence of neonatal hypothermia in Uganda: a randomized, controlled trial." *Acta Paediatr* 94.10 (2005): 1462-7.

[48] Akinbi, H, V Narendran, A Pass, P Markart, & S Hoath. "Host defense proteins in vernix caseosa and amniotic fluid." *American Journal of Obstetrics and Gynecology* 191.6 (2004): 2090–2096.

[49] Falcao, R. "Midwife Informed Consent for Vitamin K." *Gentle Birth.* Ronnie Falcao. Web. 04 Jan. 2012. <http://gentlebirth.org/archives/vitKvgf.html>.

[50] American Academy of Pediatrics Committee on Fetus and Newborn. "Controversies concerning vitamin K and the newborn." *Pediatrics.* 2003 112.1 (2003): 191-2.

[51] iBid.

[52] Monson, Kristi. "Erythromycin Side Effects." Antibiotics Home Page. Cinaero, Inc., 25 Jan. 2010. Web. 07 Mar. 2011. <http://antibiotics.emedtv.com/erythromycin/erythromycin-side-effects.html>.

[53] Peleg, D, A Steiner. "The Gomco Circumcision: Common Problems and Solutions." *American Family Physician* 58.4 (1998): 891-898.

[54] *Report 10 of the Council of Scientific Affairs (I-99): Neonatal Circumcision.* AMERICAN MEDICAL ASSOCIATION, Chicago, Illinois,
Approved by the Council on Scientific Affairs, December 1999;
published on the web, July 6, 2000. Retrieved on web 12/21/11.
<http://www.cirp.org/library/statements/ama2000/#n5>

[55] Plotkin, S, E Mortimer. *Vaccines.* Philadelphia: WB Saunders, 1994. Print.

[56] Alderson, M. *International Mortality Statistics* (Washington, DC: Facts on File, 1981), 182-183.

[57] Trollfors, B, E Rabo. "Whooping cough in adults." *British Medical Journal* 283 (1981): 696-697.

[58] Sears, R. *The Vaccine Book.* New York: Little, Brown and Company, 2007. Print.

[59] Bishop, N, R Morley, J Day, A Lucas. "Aluminum neurotoxicity in preterm infants receiving intravenous feeding solutions." *New England Journal of Medicine* 336.22 (1997): 1557-1561.

[60] Fay KE, Lai J, Bocchini JA Jr. "Update on childhood and adolescent immunizations: selected review of US recommendations and literature: part 1 & 2." *Curr Opin Pediatr.* 23.4 (2011): 460-9.

[61] "Vaccine Safety Tips for Parents." *National Vaccine Information Center – Vaccine Watch Dog.* National Vaccine Information Center. Web. 04 Jan. 2012.
<http://www.nvic.org/VaccineSafetyTips.aspx>.

[62] Vitamin C and Forced Vaccination: Neutralizing Toxicity While Optimizing Response. Dir. Thomas Levy. Vitamin C and Forced Vaccination: Neutralizing Toxicity While Optimizing Response. Fred Bloem, MD, 11/9/09. Web 9/7/11
<http://www.drbloem.com/video/vitamin-c-and-forced-vaccination.htm>

[63] Zand, J, R Walton, B Rountree. Smart Medicine for a Healthier Child: a Practical A-to-z Reference to Natural and Conventional Treatments for Infants & Children. Garden City Park, NY: Avery Pub. Group, 1994. Print.

[64] Brubaker, L, et all. "Sexual function 6 months after first delivery". *Obstet Gynecol* 11.5 (2008): 1040-4.

[65] Kendall-Tackett KA. Depression in New Mothers: Causes, Consequences and Treatment Options. Binghamton, Haworth Press: 2005.

Touch

[1] Stack, D, D Muir. "Adult tactile stimulation during face-to-face interactions modulates 5-months-olds' affect and attention." *Child Development* 63 (1992): 1509–1525.

[2] Luby, J et al. "Maternal Support in Early Childhood Predicts Larger Hippocampal Volumes At School Age." *PNAS* 109.8 (2012): 2854-2859.

[3] Klaus, M. "Mother and infant: early emotional ties." *Pediatrics.* 102.5 (1998): 1244-6.

[4] Bourne, V, B Todd. "When left means right: an explanation of the left cradling bias in terms of right hemisphere specializations." *Developmental Science* 7.1 (2004): 19-24.

[5] Salk, L. "The Effects of the Normal Heartbeat Sound on the Behavior of the Newborn Infant: Implications for Mental Health." *World Mental Health*, 12 (1960): 1-8.

[6] Freud, A. (1965). Normality and Pathology in Childhood. New York: International Universities Press.

[7] Salk, L. "The Effects of the Normal Heartbeat Sound on the Behavior of the Newborn Infant: Implications for Mental Health." *World Mental Health*, 12 (1960): 1-8.

[8] Field T, M Diego, M Hernandez-Reif. "Preterm infant massage therapy research: a review." *Infant Behav Dev.* 33.2 (2010): 115-24.

[9] Main, M, J Stadtman. "Infant Response to Rejection of Physical Contact by the Mother." Journal of the American Academy of Child Psychiatry. 20.2 (1981): 292-307.

[10] "Karina Dyer." E-mail interview. 24 Oct. 2011.

[11] Ahnert L et al. "Transition to Child Care: Associations with Infant-mother Attachment, Infant Negative Emotion, and Cortisol Elevations." *Child Development* 75.3 (2004): 649-650.

[12] Rao, MR, R Brenner, E Schisterman, T Vik, J Mills. "Long term cognitive development in children with prolonged crying." *Arch Dis Child* 89 (2004): 989-992.

[13] Gigante, J. *First Exposure to Pediatrics.* New York: McGraw-Hill, Medical Pub. Division, 2006. Print.

[14] Taubman, B. "Clinical Trial of the Treatment of Colic by Modification of Parent-Infant Interaction." *Pediatrics* 74.6 (1984): 998 -1003

[15] Bramson, L, et al. "Effect of early skin-to-skin mother infant contact during the first three hours following birth on exclusive breastfeeding during the maternity hospital stay." *Journal of Human Lactation* 26.2 (2010): 130-37.

[16] Moore, E, G Anderson, N Bergman. "Early skin-to-skin contact for mothers and their healthy newborn infants." *Cochrane Database of Systematic Review* 3 (2007).

[17] Anisfeld, E, V Casper, M Nozyce, N Cunningham. "Does Infant Carrying Promote Attachment? An Experimental Study of the Effects of Increased Physical Contact on the Development of Attachment." *Child Development* 61.5 (1990): 1617–1627.

[18] Field T, M Diego, M Hernandez-Reif. "Preterm infant massage therapy research: a review." *Infant Behav Dev* 33.2 (2010): 115-24.

[19] Small, M. Our Babies, Ourselves: How Biology and Culture Shape the Way We Parent. Anchor Books, 1998

[20] Peters KL. "Bathing premature infants: physiological and behavioral consequences." *Am J Crit Care.* 7.2 (1998): 90-100.

[21] Gee, R. "Oestrogenic and androgenic activity of triclosan in breast cancer cells." *Journal of Applied Toxicology* 28 (2008): 78–91

[22] Anderson, R, J Anderson. "Acute toxic effects of fragrance products." *Arch Environ health* 53.2 (1998): 138-146.

[23] Weinhold, B. "Environmental Factors in Birth Defects: What We Need to Know." *Environmental Health Perspective* 117.10 (2009): 440-449.

[24] US Department of Health and Human Services. 12th Report on Carcinogens, June 10, 2011. Retrieved via web 1/2/12 <http://ntp.niehs.nih.gov/?objectid=03C9AF75-E1BF-FF40-DBA9EC0928DF8B15.>

[25] Hunziker, U, R Barr. "Increased carrying reduces infant crying: a randomized controlled trial." *Pediatrics.* 77.5 (1986): 641-8.

[26] Ewold, F. "Babywearing: Bonding Love for a Lifetime." Babywearing Institute, 2009. Print.

[27] Zeedyk, MS. What's Life in a Baby Buggy Like?: The Impact of Buggy Orientation on Parent-infant Interaction and Infant Stress. National Literacy Trust. University of Dundee School of Psychology, 21 Nov. 2008. Web. 16 Aug. 2011.
<http://www.literacytrust.org.uk/assets/0000/2531/Buggy_research.pdf

Milk

[1] Goldman, AS. "The immune system of human milk: antimicrobial, antiinflammatory and immunomodulating properties [review]." *Pediatric Infect Dis J* 12 (1993): 664 -672.

[2] Lucas, A, R Morley, TJ Cole, G Lister, C Leeson-Payne "Breast Milk and Subsequent Intelligence Quotient in Children Born Preterm." *The Lancet* 339.8788 (1992): 261-264.

[3] Baumgartner, C. "Psychomotor and Social Development of Breast Fed and Bottle Fed babies During their First year of Life," *Acta Paediatr Hung* 25.4 (1984): 409-17.

[4] Marasco, L. "American Academy of Pediatrics Policy Statement on Breastfeeding and the use of Human Milk." *Pediatrics* 100.6 (1997): 1035-39.

[5] Page, D. "Breastfeeding is early functional jaw orthopedics (an introduction)." *Functional Orthodontics* 18.3 (2001): 24-27.

[6] Newcomb, P. et al. "Lactation and a reduced risk of premenopausal breast cancer." *New Engl J Med* 330 (1994): 81-87

[7] "Birth Control by Breastfeeding." *Breastfeeding.com - Everything for the New Mom*. The Bump, 2008. Web. 05 Jan. 2012.
<http://www.breastfeeding.com/reading_room/lam_page2.html>.

[8] O'Quinn, Jennifer. "Natural Child Spacing and Breastfeeding." *LEAVEN* 34.6 (98/99): 128. *La Leche League International*. Web. 5 Dec. 2011.
<http://www.llli.org/llleaderweb/lv/lvdec98jan99p128.html>.

[9] Duijts, L, V Jaddoe, A Hofman and H Moll. "Prolonged and Exclusive Breastfeeding Reduces the Risk of Infectious Diseases in Infancy." *Pediatrics* 126.8 (2010).
Le Huërou-Luron, I, S Blat, G Boudry. "Breast- v. formula-feeding: impacts on the digestive tract and immediate and long-term health effects. *Nutr Res Rev*. 23.1 (2010): 23-36.
Wold, A, I Alderberth. "Breast feeding and the intestinal microflora of the infant-- implications for protection against infectious diseases." *Adv Exp Med Biol*. 478(2000):77-93.

[10] Greer, FR, S Sicherer, A Burks. "Effects of early nutritional interventions on the development of atopic disease in infants and children: the role of maternal dietary restriction, breastfeeding, timing of introduction of complementary foods, and hydrolyzed formulas." *Pediatrics* 121.1 (2008): 183-91.
Halken, S. "Prevention of allergic disease in childhood: clinical and epidemiological aspects of primary and secondary allergy prevention." *Pediatr Allergy Immunol*. 15.16 (2004): 4-5, 9-32.
Vaarala, O, M Knip, J Paronen, et al. "Cow's milk formula feeding induces primary immunization to insulin in infants at genetic risk for Type 1 diabetes." *Diabetes* 48 (1999): 1389–1394
Host A. "Importance of the first meal on the development of cow's milk allergy and intolerance." *Allergy Proc* 12 (1991): 227–232.

[11] Riordan, Jan. *Breastfeeding and Human Lactation*. Sudbury, MA: Jones and Bartlett, 2004. p 438.

[12] Howard, C et al. "The Effects of Early Pacifier Use on Breastfeeding Duration." *Pediatrics* 103:3 e33 (1999).

[13] Gunther, M. "Instinct and the nursing couple." *Lancet* 1 (1955): 575– 578.

[14] Iacovou, Maria, and Almudena Sevilla. "Infant Feeding: The Effects of Scheduled vs. On-demand Feeding on Mothers' Wellbeing and Children's Cognitive Development." European Journal of Public Health (2012). Web. 27 Mar. 2012.
<http://eurpub.oxfordjournals.org/content/early/2012/03/13/eurpub.cks012.abstract>.

[15] Ruowei, L, S Fein, L Grummer-Strawn. "Do Infants Fed From Bottles Lack Self-regulation of Milk Intake Compared With Directly Breastfed Infants?" *Pediatrics;* published online May 10, 2010. DOI: 10.1542/peds.2009-2549.

[16] Bonyata, Kelly. "Forceful Let-down (Milk Ejection Reflex) & Oversupply." *KellyMom Breastfeeding and Parenting*. 3/29/10. Retrieved via web 1/2/12 < http://kellymom.com/bf/supply/fast-letdown.html>.

[17] "Breastfeeding: Data: NIS | DNPAO | CDC." *Centers for Disease Control and Prevention*. USA.gov, 1 Aug. 2011. Web. 06 Jan. 2012. <http://www.cdc.gov/breastfeeding/data/nis_data/>.

[18] U.S. Department of Health and Human Services. The Surgeon General's Call to Action to Support Breastfeeding. Washington, DC: U.S. Department of Health and Human Services, Office of the Surgeon General; 2011.

[19] Montgomery, D, P Splett. "Economic benefit of breast-feeding infants enrolled in WIC." *Am J Diet Assoc* 97 (1997): 379-385.

[20] Benson, J, M Masor. *Endocrine Regulations*. March 1994.

[21] Bradley, David. "Melamine in milk." *Sciencebase*. 17 September 2008. Retrieved 2011-08-30.

[22] Kyle, D, S Reeb, V Sicotte. Infant Formula and Baby Food Containing Docosahexaenoic Acid Obtained From Dinoflagellates. Martek Biosciences Corporation, assignee. Patent 5397591. 14 Mar. 1995. Print.

[23] Badger, T, J Gilchrist, R Pivik, A Andres, K Shankar, J Chen, and M. J Ronis. "The health implications of soy infant formula." *Am J Clin Nutr*, 89.5 (2009): 1668S - 1672S.

[24] [24] American Academy of Pediatrics. Committee on Nutrition. "Soy protein-based formulas: recommendations for use in infant feeding." *Pediatrics* 101.1 (1998): 148-53.

[25] Dettwyler, Kathy. "Breastfeeding Court Letter." *Welcome to Kathy Dettwyler's Home Page*. 22 Mar. 2004. Web. 05 Jan. 2012. http://www.kathydettwyler.org/detletter.htm.

[26] Pisacane, A, De Vizia B Valiante A, Vaccaro F, Russo M, Grillo G, Giustardi A. "Iron status in breast-fed infants." *Pediatrics* 127.3 (1995): 429-31.

[27] Ferguson, D et al. "Breastfeeding and subsequent social adjustment in 6-8 year-old children." *J Child Psychol Psychiatr Allied Discip* 28 (1987): 378-86.

[28] Layde, P, L Webster, A Baughman, P Wingo, G Rubin, H Ory. "The cancer and steroid hormone study group: The independent associations of parity, age at first full term pregnancy, and duration of breastfeeding with the risk of breast cancer." *Journal of Clinical Epidemiology* 42.10 (1989): 963-973,

[29] "WHO | 10 Facts on Breastfeeding." *World Health Organization*. July 2011. Web. 06 Jan. 2012. <http://www.who.int/features/factfiles/breastfeeding/en/>.

[30] Rosenblatt, KA, DB Thomas, and the WHO collaborative study of neoplasia and steroid contraceptives. "Prolonged Lactation and endometrial cancer." *Int J Epidemiol* 24 (1995): 499-503.

[31] Blaauw, R. et al. "Risk factors for development of osteoporosis in a South African population." *South African Medical Journal*. 84 (1994): 328-32

[32] Karlson, EW, LA Mandl, SE Hankinson, F Grodstein. "Do breast-feeding and other reproductive factors influence future risk of rheumatoid arthritis?" *Arthritis Rheum*. 50.11 (2004): 3458-67.

Sleep

[1] McKenna, J. Manuscript review. 11 Nov. 2011.

[2] Johnston, J, J Amico. "A prospective longitudinal study of the release of oxytocin and prolactin in response to infant suckling in long term lactation." *J Clin Endrocinol Metab* 62 (1986): 653–657.

[3] "Sleeping through the Night." *Welcome to Kathy Dettwyler's Home Page*. 25 Aug. 1997. Web. 06 Apr. 2011.
<http://www.kathydettwyler.org/detsleepthrough.html>. April 20, 2011.

[4] Thompson, R. "Emotion regulation: A theme in search of definition." *Monographs of the Society for Research in Child Development* 59 (1994): 25-52.

[5] Gottman J, L Katz, C Hooven. "Parental meta-emotion philosophy and the emotional life of families: Theoretical models and preliminary data." *Journal of Family Psychology* 10 (1996): 243-268.

[6] Stickgold, R et al. "Sleep, Learning, and Dreams: Off-line Memory Reprocessing" *Science* 5544 (2001): 1052-1057.

[7] Maquet, P. "The Role of Sleep in Learning and Memory." *Science*. 5544 (2001): 1048-1052.

[8] Walker, M, T Brakefield, A Morgan, J Hobson, R Stickgold. "Practice with Sleep Makes Perfect: Sleep-Dependent Motor Skill Learning." *Neuron* 35.1 (2002): 205-211.

[9] Narvaez, Darcia. "Early Experience, Human Nature and Moral Development." 2010 Notre Dame Symposium on Human Development and Early Experience. Notre Dame University, South Bend. 3 Feb. 2011. Presentation.

[10] Gettler, L, J McKenna. "Never Sleep with Baby? Or Keep Me Close But Keep Me Safe: Eliminating Inappropriate 'Safe Infant Sleep' Rhetoric in the United States" *Current Pediatric Reviews* 6.1 (2010): 71-77. (refereed)

[11] Consumer Safety Product Commission. "CPSC Warns Against Placing Babies in Adult Beds; Study finds 64 deaths each year from suffocation and strangulation." September 29, 1999. http://www.cpsc.gov/cpscpub/prerel/prhtml99/99175.html> Retrieved 1/2/12.

[12] Deaths: Final data [for 1996-2005]. 1998-2008. National Vital Statistics Reports; vols 47-56. Hyattsville, Maryland: National Center for Health Statistics.

[13] "Home Page." *American Sudden Infant Death Syndrome Institute* Web. 06 Apr. 2011. <http://www.sids.org>.

[14] Waynforth, D. "The influence of parent–infant co-sleeping, nursing, and childcare on cortisol and SlgA immunity in a sample of British children." *Developmental Psychobiology* 49.6 (2007): 640–648. Print.

[15] Davies, L "Babies co-sleeping with parents" *Midwives* 108.1295(1995)384-6.

[16] iBid.

[17] McKenna, J, T McDade. "Why Babies Should Never Sleep Alone: A Review of the Cosleeping Controversy In Relationship To SIDS, Breast Feeding and Bedsharing." *Paediatric Respiratory Reviews* 6.2 (2005): 134-152.

[18] iBid.

[19] Gettler, L, J McKenna. "Never Sleep with Baby? Or Keep Me Close But Keep Me Safe: Eliminating Inappropriate 'Safe Infant Sleep' Rhetoric in the United States." *Current Pediatric Reviews* 6.1 (2010): 71-77. (refereed)

[20] Forbes, F, D Weiss, R Folen. "The co-sleeping habits of military children." *Military Medicine*. 157.4 (1992): 196-200.

Lewis, R, L Janda. "The relationship between adult sexual adjustment and childhood experience regarding exposure to nudity, sleeping in the parental bed, and parental attitudes toward sexuality." *Archives of Sexual Behavior* 17 (1988): 349–363.

Okami, P, T Weisner, R Olmstead. "Outcome correlates of parent-child bedsharing: an eighteen-year longitudinal study." *Journal of Developmental and Behavioral Pediatrics* 23.4 (2002): 244–254.

Crawford, M. "Parenting practices in the Basque country: implications of infant and childhood sleeping location for personality development." *Ethos* 22.1 (1994): 42–82.

Mosenkis, J. "The effects of childhood co-sleeping on later life development." MSc thesis: Department of Cultural Psychology, The University of Chicago, 1998.

[21] Ball, HL. "Breastfeeding, bedsharing, and infant sleep." *Birth* 30 (2003): 181–188.

[22] Cigarette Smoking Among Adults and Trends in Smoking Cessation—US, 2008. MMWR. 58.44 (2009): 1227-1232. Retrieved on Web, 1/3/11.
<http://www.cdc.gov/mmwr/preview/mmwrhtml/mm5844a2.htm>

[23] "Indoor Air Pollution: An Introduction for Health Professionals. Indoor Air Quality. US EPA." *US Environmental Protection Agency.* 4 Nov. 2010. Web. 11 Mar. 2011.
<http://www.epa.gov/iaq/pubs/hpguide.html>.

[24] Stapleton, H, S Klosterhaus, A Keller, P Ferguson, S van Bergen, E Cooper, T Webster, and A Blum. "Identification of Flame Retardants in Polyurethane Foam Collected from Baby Products." *Environmental Science and Technology* 45.12 (2011): 5323-5331.

[25] Faust, J, L Meehan August. *EVIDENCE ON THE CARCINOGENICITY OF TRIS(1,3-DICHLORO-2-PROPYL) PHOSPHATE.".* Rep. C. *Office of Environmental Health Hazard Assessment.* California Environmental Protection Agency, July 2011. Web. 17 June 2011.
<http://www.oehha.ca.gov/prop65/hazard_ident/pdf_zip/TDCPP070811.pdf>.

[1] Dioxins and their effects on human health. World Health Organization. May 2010. Fact Sheet No. 225. Retrieved on web 12/31/2011.
<http://www.who.int/mediacentre/factsheets/fs225/en/>

[2] Partsch, C, Aukamp, M, Sippell, W. "Scrotal temperature is increased in disposable plastic lined nappies." *Arch Dis Child* 83 (2000): 364-368.

[3] Anderson, R and J. "Acute respiratory effects of diaper emissions. *Arch Environ Health* 54.5(1999): 353-8.

[4] Armstrong, L, Scott, A. Whitewash: Exposing the Health and Environmental Dangers of Women's Sanitary Products and Disposable Diapers: What You Can Do about It. Toronto: HarperPerennial, 1992. Print.

[5] Ibid.

[6] Lehrburger, C, Mullen, J and Jones, C. *Diapers: Environmental Impacts and Lifecycle Analysis.* Philadelphia, PA: Report to The National Association of Diaper Services (NADS). 1991.

[7] Blum, N, et al. "Relationship between age at initiation of toilet training and duration of training: A prospective study." *Pediatrics* 111.4 (2003): 810-814.

Relate

[1] Ainsworth, M, J Bowlby. "Research Strategy in the Study of Mother-Child Separation." *Courrier* 4 (1954): 105-131.

[2] Brazelton, T Berry. *To Listen to a Child: Understanding the Normal Problems of Growing Up.* USA: Perseus Publishing, 1984.

[3] Capiric, O et al. "Teaching sign language to hearing children as a possible factor in cognitive enhancement." J. *Deaf Stud & Deaf Educ* 3 (1998): 2-8.

[4] Hirsh-Pasek, K, R Golinkoff, D Eyer. Einstein Never Used Flash Cards: How Our Children Really Learn-- And Why They Need to Play More and Memorize Less. PA: Rodale Books, 2003.

[5] Ginsburg, K. "The Importance of Play in Promoting Health Child Development and Maintaining Strong Parent-Child Bonds." *Pediatrics* 119.1 (1997): 182-191.

[6] Christakis, D et al. "Early Television Exposure and Subsequent Attentional Problems in Children." *Pediatrics* 113.4 (2004): 708-713.

Eat

[1] "Experts seek to debunk baby food myths: Little evidence supports 'any particular way of doing things.'" *MSNBC*. MSNBC, 9 October 2005. Web. 17 April 2011. http://www.msnbc.msn.com/id/9646449/ns/health-kids_and_parenting.

[2] "Experts Seek to Debunk Baby Food Myths - Health - Children's Health - Msnbc.com."*Msnbc.com - Breaking News, Science and Tech News, World News, US News, Local News- Msnbc.com.* 9 Oct. 2005. Web. 01 Feb. 2011.<http://www.msnbc.msn.com/id/9646449/ns/health-childrens_health/t/experts-seek-debunk-baby-food-myths/>.

[3] Rapley, G, T Murkett. Baby Led Weaning: The Essential Guide to Introducing Solid Foods - and Helping Your Baby to Grow Up a Happy and Confident Eater. London: The Experiment, 2010.

[4] Kull, I, M Wickman, G Lilja, S Nordvall, G Pershagen. "Breast feeding and allergic diseases in infants—a prospective birth cohort study." *Archives of Diseases in Childhood* 87 (2002): 478-481.

[5] Fox, M, B Devaney, K Reidy, C Razafindrakoto, P Ziegler. "Relationship between portion size and energy intake among infants and toddlers: evidence of self-regulation." *Journal of the American Dietetic Association* 106 (2006): S77-83.

[6] Macknin, M, S Medendorp, M Maier. "Infant sleep and bedtime cereal."*Am J Dis Child* 143.9 (1989): 1066–1068.

[7] Branum, A, and S Lukacs. Issue brief no. 10. *Food Allergy Among U.S. Children: Trends in Prevalence and Hospitalization.* U.S. Department of Health and Human Services, Oct. 2008. Web. 28 Oct. 2011. <http://www.sflorg.com/comm_center/medical/pdf/637_48_01.pdf>.

[8] iBid.

[9] De Filippo, C. "Impact of Diet in Shaping Gut Microbiota Revealed by a Comparative Study in Children from Europe and Rural Africa."*Proceedings of the National Academy of Science* 107 (2010). Web. 5 Sept. 2011. <http://www.pnas.org/content/early/2010/07/14/1005963107>.

[10] Du Toit, G et al. "Early consumption of peanuts in infancy is associated with a low prevalence of peanut allergy." *The Journal of Allergy and Clinical Immunology* 122 (2008): 984-991.

[11] Greer, F, S Sicherer, A Wesley Burks. "Effects of Early Nutritional Interventions on the Development of Atopic Disease in Infants and Children: The Role of Maternal Dietary Restriction, Breastfeeding, Timing of Introduction of Complementary Foods, and Hydrolyzed Formulas." *Pediatrics* 121.1 (2008): 183-191.

[12] Bonang, G, H Monintja, Sujudi, D van der Waaij. "Influence of breastmilk on the development of resistance to intestinal colonization in infants born at the Atma Jaya Hospital, Jakarta." *Scandinavian Journal of Infectious Disease* 32 (2000): 189-96.

[13] Lustig, Robert. "Childhood obesity: behavioral aberration or biochemical drive? Reinterpreting the First Law of Thermodynamics" Nature Clinical Practice Endocrinology & Metabolism 2 (2006): 447-458.

[14] Vasanti, S. et al."Sugar-Sweetened Beverages and Risk of Metabolic Syndrome and Type 2 Diabetes: A meta-analysis." *Diabetes Care* 33.11 (2010): 2477-2483.

[15] Cornee, J et al. "A Case-control Study of Gastric Cancer and Nutritional Factors in Marseille, France," *European Journal of Epidemiology* 11 (95): 55-65.

[16] Reiser, S. "Effects of Dietary Sugars on Metabolic Risk Factors Associated with Heart Disease." *Nutritional Health* (1985): 203-216.

[17] Jones, TW et al. "Enhanced Adrenomedullary Response and Increased Susceptibility to Neuroglygopenia: Mechanisms Underlying the adverse effect of Sugar Ingestion in Children." *Journal of Pediatrics* 126 (1995): pp 171-177.

[18] Davis, C. "Attention-deficit/Hyperactivity Disorder: Associations with Overeating and Obesity." *Current Psychiatry Reports* 12.5 (2010): 389–395.

[19] Johnson, RK. "Dietary Sugar Intake and Cardiovascular Health." *Circulation* 120 (2009): 1011-1020.

[20] Davis C. "Results of the self-selection of diets by young children." *Canadian Medical Association Journal* 41 (1939): 257-61.

[21] Midur, T. "Update: infant botulism." *Clinical Microbiology Reviews* 9.2 (1996) 119–125.

[22] Elobeid, M, D Allison. "Putative environmental-endocrine disruptors and obesity: a review." *Current opinion in endocrinology, diabetes, and obesity* 15.5 (2008): 403–408.

[23] Jones, D, G Miller. "The effects of environmental neurotoxicants on the dopaminergic system: A possible role in drug addiction". *Biochemical pharmacology* 76.5 (2008): 569–581.

[24] Bucher, J, M Shelby. "Since You Asked - Bisphenol A(BPA)." *National Institute of Environmental Health Sciences (NIEHS)*. Web. 06 May 2011. <http://www.niehs.nih.gov/news/sya/sya-bpa/>.

[25] The Endocrine Society. "BPA lowers male fertility, mouse study finds." *ScienceDaily*, 6 Jun. 2011. Web. 22 Nov. 2011.

[26] Sugiura-ogasawara, M, Ozaki, Y, Sonta, S, Makino, T, Suzumori, K. "Exposure to bisphenol A is associated with recurrent miscarriage". *Human reproduction (Oxford, England)* 20.8 (2005): 2325–2329.

[27] Brisken, C. "Endocrine Disruptors and Breast Cancer." *CHIMIA International Journal for Chemistry* 62.5 (2008): 406–409

[28] iBid.

[29] Wilding, B, et al. Rep. *No Silver Lining-An Investigation into Bisphenol A in Canned Foods*. National Workgroup for Safe Markets, 18 May 2010. Web. 13 May 2011. <http://bit.ly/wtVowl>.

[30] Kuroto-Niwa, R, et al. "Estrogenic activity of alkylphenols, bisphenol S, and their chlorinated derivatives using a GFP expression system." *Environmental Toxicology and Pharamacology* 19.1 (2005): 121-130.

[31] Perez, P, R Pulgar, F Olea-Serrano, M Villalobos, A Rivas, M Metzler, V Pedraza, N Olea. "The estrogenicity of bisphenol A-related diphenylalkanes with various substituents at the central carbon and the hydroxy groups." *Environmental Health Perspectives* 106.3 (1998): 167-174.

[32] Hardell, L, C Ohlson, M Fredrikson. "Occupational Exposure to Polyvinyl Chloride as a Risk Factor for Testicular Cancer Evaluated in a Case-control Study." *International Journal of Cancer* 73.6 (1997): 828-30.

[33] Rep. *Third National Report on Human Exposure to Environmental Chemicals*. Department of Health and Human Services Centers for Disease Control and Prevention, July 2005. Web. 18 July 2011. <http://www.cphfoundation.org/documents/thirdreport_001.pdf>.

[34] Lovekamp-Swan, T, B Davis. "Mechanisms of phthalate ester toxicity in the female reproductive system." *Environmental Health Perspectives* 111.2 (2003): 139–45.

[35] Thornton, J. *Environmental Impacts of Polyvinyl Chloride (PVC) Building Materials*. Rep. Washington D.C.: Healthy Building Network, 2002. Nov. 2002. Web. 5 Jan. 2011. <http://www.healthybuilding.net/pvc/Thornton_Enviro_Impacts_of_PVC.pdf

36 "Risks of Plastic Chemical Add Up for Infants" Environmental Working Group, February 2008. Web. 9 Mar. 2012. <http://www.ewg.org/node/26052>.

37 Houlihan, J. "Canaries in the Kitchen: Teflon Toxicosis" Environmental Working Group, May 2003. Web. 16 Mar. 2011. <http://www.ewg.org/reports/toxicteflon>.

Index

Made in the USA
Monee, IL
04 January 2020

19854611R00116